LIFE AFTER PET LOSS

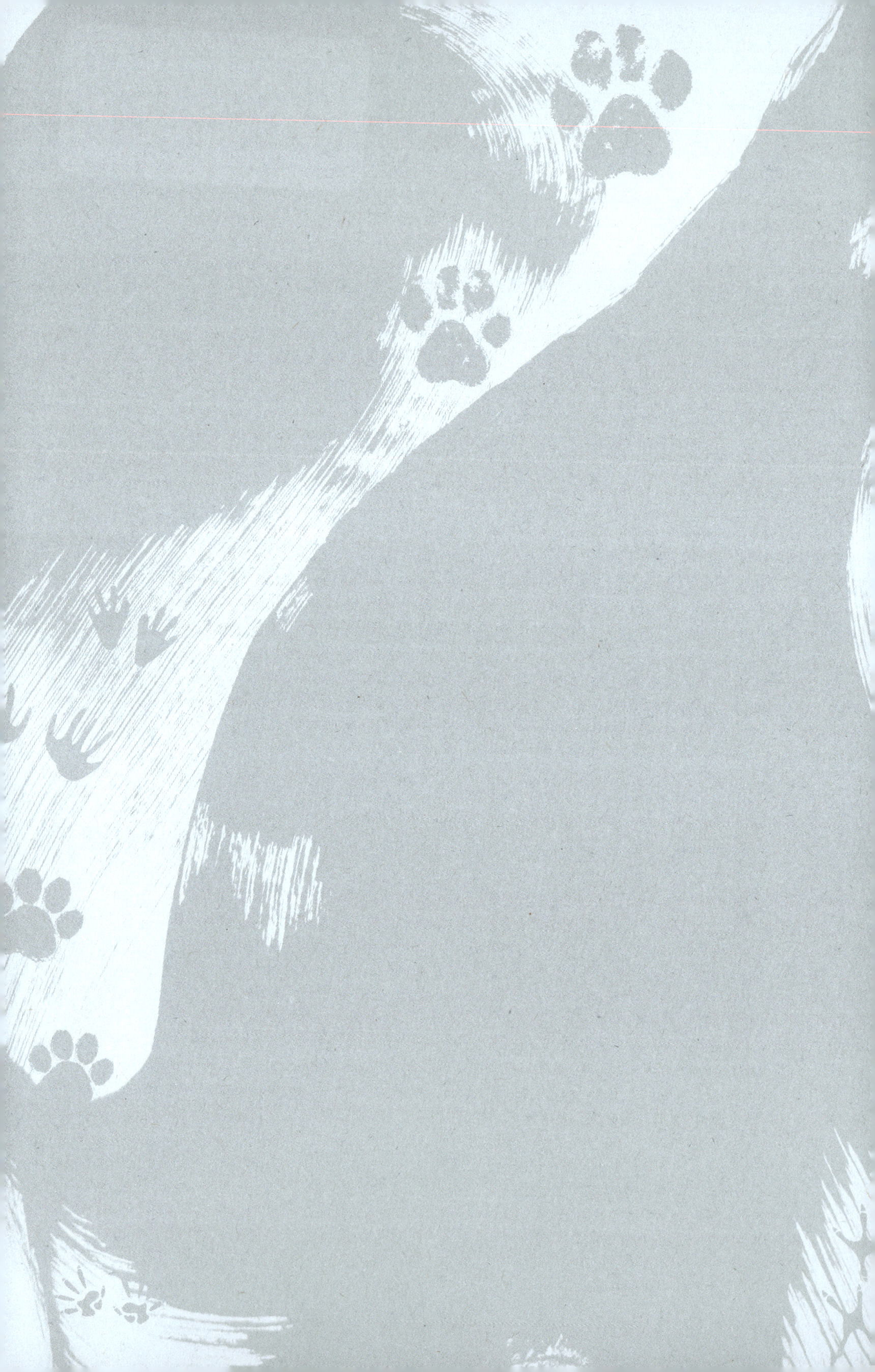

Daily Reflections for
Working Through Grief

Life After Pet Loss

JUDITH EVE ROSEN, LCSW

Zeitgeist • New York

Zeitgeist™
An imprint and division of Penguin Random House LLC
1745 Broadway, New York, NY 10019
zeitgeistpublishing.com
penguinrandomhouse.com

ISBN: 9798217151073
Ebook ISBN: 9798217151066

Printed in the United States of America
1st Printing

Illustrations © by Shutterstock.com/Polina Raulina, Shutterstock.com/KatarinaF, Shutterstock.com/SantaLiza
Book design by Emma Hall
Author photograph © by Johnny Rodriguez
Edited by Erin Nelson

The authorized representative in the EU for product safety and compliance is Penguin Random House Ireland, Morrison Chambers, 32 Nassau Street, Dublin D02 YH68, Ireland. https://eu-contact.penguin.ie

For my sweet cat Joni, my love for you inspired me to become a veterinary social worker. You will always be snuggled, in my heart.

INTRODUCTION

Welcome, dear reader. I am both glad and sorry that you're here. The recent or imminent loss of a pet can feel overwhelming and complicated. In my work, clients are often shocked by the degree of their pain. I'm here to validate the depth of your grief. Love is love. When you lose a companion who means something to you, it hurts—regardless of their form.

Perhaps you are feeling some, or all, of the following:

* You can't imagine life without your beloved animal companion. Saying goodbye feels heavy and dark.
* There's a giant hole in your heart. You wonder how you will ever fill it.
* Friends and family tell you that your baby "is in a better place" or that you will "move on" in a few weeks. While they may mean well, this invalidates and exacerbates your pain.
* You don't know how to ask for time off to grieve; your colleagues might think your beloved was "just a pet."
* You have never felt so alone.

I have had to say goodbye to three beloved cats, most recently my sweet Joni in 2018. She passed away only three months after my mother, and I was devastated by the compounded losses.

The veterinarian let me sit with Joni during her passing. I was able to pet her and speak softly to her as the sedative took effect. I wanted the last touch and sound she experienced to be mine. When the procedure was over,

I turned to the veterinarian and the vet technician and said, "She's with my mom now, curled up in her lap and sleeping."

The three of us cried together.

I decided the best way to honor Joni's memory was to help others who are experiencing similar grief. So I enrolled in the veterinary social work certificate program at the University of Tennessee and have been guiding people like you through this process ever since.

This book offers comfort and support to those who've loved and lost any pet—from the tiniest mouse to the grandest stallion. Throughout the course of your healing journey, let yourself be grounded by this universal truth: Grief looks different for everyone. There's no "normal" timeline for grieving, and no "right" or "wrong" way to grieve. You may feel strong emotions, a mix of conflicting emotions, or no emotion at all. The intensity of your emotions may ebb and flow, like waves in the ocean.

Grief may also show up differently for you depending on the day, the week, the year, even the hour or minute. Some days all you will want to talk about is how much it hurts. Other days, you will want to distract yourself and avoid the matter altogether. Both extremes—and everything in between—are normal reactions to losing a loved one. They are all okay.

I hope to guide you through the distinct pain of pet loss, however it may manifest for you. There are 365 entries—one for each day of the year. Feel free to pull from whatever page resonates with you at any given moment. Start on any day you wish. Go in chronological order or skip around. Entries are dated for the sole purpose of giving you a way in.

The book is grounded in comfort and practicality. Entries alternate between a comforting quote and reflection, and a practical action or tip to help you move through—and with—the grieving process. You can modify the tips or activities to suit your situation. Take what works and skip the rest. If anything feels too overwhelming, allow yourself a break or move on. You can always go back to it later if you like.

At the end of each entry, you'll find an affirmation. If the affirmation rings true for you, consider saying that affirmation a few times during the day. You can also reword it so it's more meaningful to you or choose not to use it at all.

There are several writing activities in the book. If these appeal to you, I suggest a designated journaling space for this purpose, be it a paper notebook or an electronic device. This way, you will have all your writings and memories in one place.

The "Resources" section at the back of the book lists pet-loss-specific support groups, books, and websites that can offer additional guidance during what may be one of the toughest moments of your life. Feel free to refer to this section at any point.

As you sift through these pages, remember that while your grief is unique, you are not alone in experiencing it. Not now, or ever. There is a whole community of people who profoundly love their animal companions and suffer deeply when they are gone. This book is for them. This book is for you.

EDITOR'S NOTE

The day I had my first phone call with Judith, I also received the news that Hendrix—our eight-year-old rescue dog—had an inoperable tumor in his intestines. *You've got the wrong dog,* I thought as the vet explained the diagnosis. *He was chasing squirrels this morning! Can't you see he's barely middle-aged?*

Three weeks later, my family made the excruciating decision to say goodbye to Hendrix. My kids sat inside with their grandmother as Hendrix rested his head in my lap, my husband sobbing nose to snout with him, while I hummed the lullaby I had sung to my children as newborns: "I've got peace like a river . . ." and he slipped away.

Hendrix was free, no longer in pain. But what were the rest of us left to do? I didn't have the sense of peace people talk about after a beloved animal crosses the rainbow bridge. I didn't feel much at all.

Then one night, sitting on the couch with a cup of tea and this book, something broke open inside me. It was the April 29th entry that lifted the floodgates—and the new reality that came with it. Hendrix was gone. He wasn't coming back. My young son likely wouldn't remember him. And my park walks and the space beneath my desk would never be the same. What would I do with his collar? Was it even possible to watch a show without his head gently perched on my thigh?

This book gave me—at an unexpected moment—an outlet for the grief that had been trapped inside. Its simple, gentle, and wise practicality became the balm to my heartbreak. I could light a candle, frame his picture, or write him a letter telling him how sorry I was for the days I was too tired to throw him the ball.

Most of all, Judith reminded me that the depth of our love—Hendrix's and mine—was real, powerful, and lasting. She understands, as both a licensed grief professional and someone who has lived through the pain of pet loss, that there is no quick fix for this grief. Instead, she offers bite-sized reminders that our love mattered, that our pets cherished each messy and profound moment with us, and that every small action we take to process this loss honors a bond that doesn't disappear but transforms.

Whether you visit these pages every day, skim them when you need them, or find yourself somewhere in between, they are here to comfort and guide you through the process of living life after pet loss.

Grief is, after all, species agnostic—and love in its most enduring form.

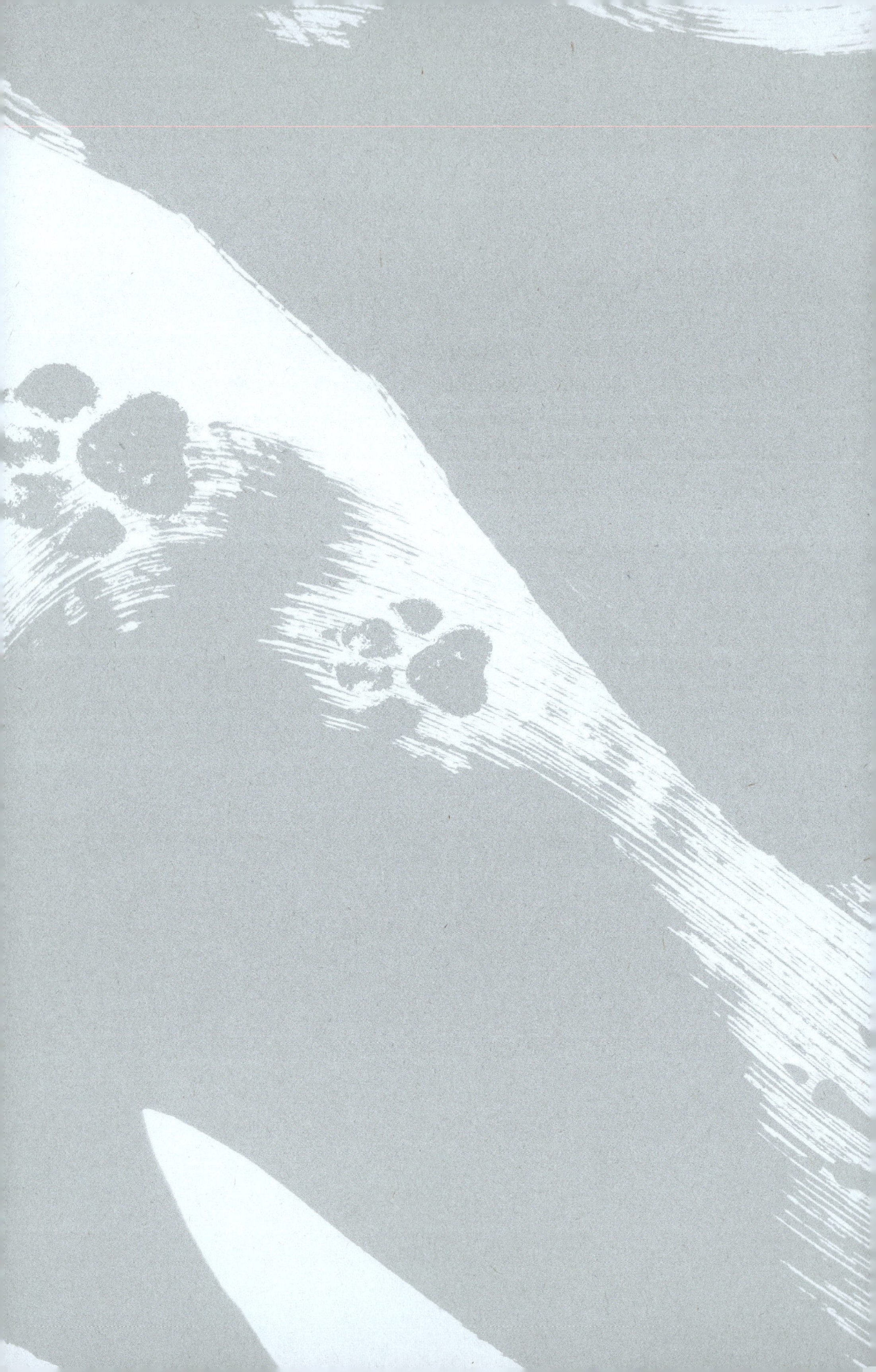

JANUARY 1

"The pain of grief is just as much a part of life as the joy of love; it is, perhaps, the price we pay for love, the cost of commitment." —COLIN MURRAY PARKES

Your pet gave you unconditional love, companionship, joy, and purpose. As you grieve, you will explore how to continue nurturing the bond you had with your pet, even if the form of that bond has changed. The heartache you feel now is a sign of just how much your pet opened up your heart while they were here. Each pang is an expression of the love you gave, and the love you received. The precious gifts they gave you will stay with you forever.

The beautiful bond we had together is unbreakable. This love is a part of who I am.

JANUARY 2

WHAT ROLES DID YOU PLAY IN YOUR PET'S LIFE? Take a moment to think about all the wonderful things you did for your pet. Remember that you were their dedicated caregiver and played many roles. Give each role an official title, like Head Nutritionist, Director of Toys, Exercise Coordinator, or Chief Treats Officer. Create a list of these roles or, if you feel up to it, create a job description with the details of your daily routines.

Caretaking is rooted in love and dedication, not perfection.

JANUARY 3

"Grief is not a bad thing. Grief is a reaction to a bad thing. Grief itself is a natural process that has to be experienced."

—STEPHEN COLBERT

Pain is the alarm system that goes off when something in your body needs attention. If you broke your ankle and didn't experience pain, you would keep walking on it, causing further injury. When you experience the loss of a being that was deeply important to you, grief is a natural emotional reaction. It signals that there's been injury, so that there may be healing. Though the pain may feel overwhelming, there are ways to ease this pain as you slowly mend. You are always in charge of when and how to do that.

My feelings are a valid and normal reaction to loss. It's part of being human.

JANUARY 4

CREATE A GRIEF JOURNAL. A grief journal is a notebook where you can record your private thoughts and feelings about your loss. Use it to tell stories about your beloved pet, be it through words, drawings, or any other artwork. The important thing is that it is uniquely yours. Some people like to write at a set time every day; others prefer to do it whenever inspiration strikes. Today, write about how you are feeling at this moment. What's going through your mind? Jot your thoughts down freely for a few minutes, without worrying about how the words come out. The intent is to connect with your emotions and begin to identify where you are in the grieving process.

I write for myself and no one else. Writing is a sacred form of catharsis.

JANUARY 5

"I ask no more than to live a hundred years longer, that I may have more time to dwell the longer on your memory."

—JULES VERNE

Talking about or writing down memories of your pet can help you maintain a deep emotional connection even if they're no longer physically present. Sharing photos and videos with others can help unearth memories, like a treasure hunt where buried jewels are gradually revealed. It's okay if you are not yet ready to delve into your memories. You may still be processing the loss. If this is the case, allow yourself that time and space.

Memories need not fade over time.

JANUARY 6

REFLECTION IS A POWERFUL TOOL FOR EMOTIONAL RECOVERY. Write a thank-you note to your beloved pet for all they brought into your life. Consider the activities you enjoyed together, how they made you feel, and what you valued most in your relationship. Create your own card or find a thank-you card that speaks to you. When you are ready, read the card out loud to your pet. While you read it, gaze at their picture, stand by their urn, or imagine them with you. Do what's most comfortable for you.

I have the ability to reflect on my love for my pet at any time.

JANUARY 7

"If, while we sleep, we can have any pleasing dreams, it is as the French say, *tante gagné,* so much added to the pleasure of life." —BENJAMIN FRANKLIN

It's not unusual for grieving people to feel their pet's "presence." They may report hearing them in the next room or feeling their weight at the foot of the bed. Some people have vivid dreams of their pet. How you interpret your dreams is personal to you. (If you don't have these dreams, that's okay, too.) If these sensations are comforting to you, embrace them. You are not alone in feeling your pet's loving presence.

I miss your warm presence next to me, and I can find ways to still connect with you.

JANUARY 8

FEEL CLOSER TO YOUR PET WITH A COMFORT OBJECT. Choose an object that belonged to your pet, such as a collar, toy, or blanket. Sit in a quiet, comfortable spot. Hold the object in your hands. If it's large, you can set it near you with your hands placed gently on top. Now, if you're comfortable doing so, close your eyes. Take three deep, relaxing breaths. Picture your pet interacting with this object. Imagine them healthy and happy. Feel the object in your hand or your lap. Connect to the memory for as long as you like. When you feel ready, take one more deep breath, wiggle your toes, and shake out your shoulders. Then, open your eyes. How do you feel? If this was helpful, keep the object nearby in case you need comfort. If at any point in this exercise you feel overwhelmed with emotion, it's okay to stop.

I allow myself to seek comfort. I accept that comfort might look different each day.

JANUARY 9

"I know now that we never get over great losses; we absorb them, and they carve us into different, often kinder, creatures." —GAIL CALDWELL

Living through grief and loss can change you in ways you may not expect. Loss can bring clarity that helps you focus on what you value most in life. You have seen how suddenly life can change. Perhaps this brings gratitude for every moment you had with your pet. Or illuminates how you want to treat others—or yourself—as you move forward. Many people who live through loss report feeling deeper empathy for others who are grieving or in pain.

I allow myself to be transformed by this experience.

JANUARY 10

MAKE A DONATION IN THEIR NAME. This can be monetary or involve unused or lightly used pet items. Making a donation will tie generosity to the memory of your pet. Consider marking your calendar to donate on a special day, such as your pet's birthday or "Gotcha Day" (the day you brought your pet home or adopted them). Animal welfare agencies, stray rescues, or local shelters can all benefit from this act of paying it forward. There is no wrong way to donate.

Generosity is never wasted.

JANUARY 11

"It's true what they say. We are their entire lives and it is the greatest shame that they can only bless us with a short spark of time in ours." —CHRISSY TEIGEN

Experiencing the loss of a pet is one of the painful realities of the human-animal bond. Depending on the species, you may have had the joy of their presence for only a few years (such as a gerbil or senior pet) or for decades (such as a cockatiel or horse). Regardless of the duration of your shared life, you are here because that connection touched you in a profound way. Although you may wish you had been able to give them more time or more attention, focus on all that you did give them, starting with how you welcomed them into your home. Thinking back on the time you spent together, starting with the day you first met, can offer some comfort as you are grieving.

I honor the time we spent together. I will love you forever.

JANUARY 12

SO HOW DID YOU TWO MEET? In Hollywood, the moment two people meet is called a meet-cute. It's often unusual, funny, or otherwise charming, foreshadowing the relationship at large. Tell the story of your meet-cute—the first time you and your pet met. Include as much detail as you can: where you were, what went through your mind, what they looked like, and how you reacted to each other. You can write a journal entry or create a scrapbook page with visuals and text. If you feel inspired, tell the story in photos, videos, or audio—whatever feels right. This exercise can serve as a cleansing release or a keepsake you visit again and again.

I cherish the uniqueness of our story. I loved you from the start.

JANUARY 13

"Part of the healing process is sharing with other people who care." —JERRY CANTRELL

Pet loss is rarely given the same emotional weight as the loss of a human family member. Most jobs don't offer bereavement leave for a pet, and people may stop checking in with you after just a few short days or weeks. Without proper acknowledgment, it may start to feel like you can't share your grief. This is called *disenfranchised grief*, and it's a lonely place to be. While it's lonely, you're not alone.

Disenfranchised grief is a common experience for those experiencing pet loss. Consider connecting with others who can relate to your specific pain by attending a pet-loss support group, calling a hotline that specializes in pet-loss grief, follow pet-loss counselors on social media, or call a friend who's had a similar loss. There is validation at the other end of this connection. Every time I lead a grief support group, I am deeply moved by the incredible outpouring of love and support the group members share. The most common feedback I hear is, "Finally, I'm with a group of people who 'get it.' I don't have to explain why I'm so sad."

I may feel lonely, but I am not alone in this grief.

JANUARY 14

FIND WAYS TO START TALKING ABOUT YOUR GRIEF. Pick two people who are good listeners. Schedule time with each of them. Tell them you consider them a great listener, and that what you need right now is for someone to just listen. They don't need to find magic words to "make you feel better" (those words don't exist), and they don't need to offer advice. You just need them to hold space for you to share in this moment.

I don't have to hold my grief alone.

JANUARY 15

"Because every relationship is so unique, no two people grieve the same way. And you have no idea how you are going to grieve till you are grieving." —ALYSIA REINER

Nobody can, or should, tell you how to grieve the loss of a beloved animal companion. You are a unique individual with your own personal history, beliefs, and values. The special connection you shared with your pet was just as unique, so the way you grieve will reflect that bond. Allow yourself to process this loss, and to create a nurturing space for yourself, in a way that works for you—and you alone. There's an element of trial and error to it, and that's to be expected. Just keep what works and toss out what doesn't. Most importantly, remember to be gentle and take your time.

My grieving process is as unique as our love was.

JANUARY 16

TAKE A BREAK WITH A PLEASANT ACTIVITY. Some days all you can think about is your loss. Other days you just want to forget that it happened. Create a list of "Things I Can Do"—these are activities you'll have on hand when you need distraction or comfort, but planning might feel too tough that day. These are easy-to-access activities that don't require much effort but can still shift your state of mind. Consider listening to your favorite playlist and singing along to your favorite song; watching a video of a comedian who really makes you laugh; going for a brisk walk; sitting in the sunshine; eating a fresh piece of fruit; or texting with a friend. Turn to this list whenever you need a low-stakes reset.

Joy can be found in even the simplest activities.

JANUARY 17

"All animals, except man, know that the principal business of life is to enjoy it." —SAMUEL BUTLER

From a mouse running on a wheel as fast as it can to a stallion galloping across the pasture, animals find joy in simple pleasures. They remind us to make time for play, interaction, and rest. There is something elemental about their existence. These lessons about balance and joy stay with us long after our animal companions exit our lives. We honor them by continuing to enjoy life every day. This is not easy grief work, but it is essential.

I honor my beloved's memory by finding moments of joy.

JANUARY 18

LIST THREE ACTIVITIES THAT BROUGHT YOUR PET UNENCUMBERED JOY. Which of their favorite pastimes bring a smile to your face right now? It can be something as simple as a belly rub or a very specific toy or game. Was there a special human or animal they were always excited to see? A comfy spot where they liked to snooze during the day? Visualizing your pet at their happiest is a way to bring warmth to your heart.

I delight in picturing you in your happiest place.

JANUARY 19

"It's been extremely painful to lose our beloved Chewie . . . She grew up with our kids and remained at our sides when each left the nest. She waited by the front door to welcome her siblings back home . . ." —KELLY RIPA

One of the reasons we bond so closely with our pets is that they are with us through major life milestones and important events. In young families, they can shepherd human siblings from infancy through adolescence, sometimes all the way out of the nest. For all of us, they are markers of time. Who we were when they arrived in our home is different from who we are by the time they leave—however long that is. We are different, in part, because of their presence and the love it fostered.

Thank you for being an important part of my life story.

JANUARY 20

CREATE A MEMORY BOX. A memory box allows you to gather mementos from your pet's life. Gather items to place in a box. Select from their favorite toys, collars, clothes, or grooming items. Include photos, holiday cards, or other memorabilia. Any time you want to feel closer and connected to them, simply open the box, pull out an item, and hold it in your hands. Please note that this can be an emotionally charged exercise. Feel free to skip it and return to it when the time feels right.

In your absence, I still feel your love.

JANUARY 21

"Upon learning of the loss, I was inconsolable and beyond devastated—until I realized Sheck imparted an important final life lesson with her departure: No Day is Promised. So never take anyone you love (or even like) for granted . . ." —KEVIN SMITH

Losing a loved one is a stark reminder that time is precious. Almost always, we long for just one more day—one more walk, pet, purr, squawk, or coo. You might feel an urge to say "I love you" to loved ones far louder and more often than you did before your loss. Living your life more fully is a way to honor your pet's memory. So is understanding that each moment counts—it is a precious gift they left with you.

I notice small glimmers of beauty today.

JANUARY 22

COMPLETE A RANDOM ACT OF KINDNESS. Random acts of kindness are powerful tools for healing. They can give you a sense of purpose and value. Buy a cup of coffee for the person behind you in line. Email a thank-you note to a former teacher or coach who made a difference in your life. The *what* is less important than the gesture of kindness behind it. Sometimes the best way to comfort yourself is by being kind to someone else.

My healing journey can positively impact others in unforeseen ways.

JANUARY 23

"I grieved for [Phiz] a long time, and resolved never to have another dog . . . Everybody knows how the proverbial other dog arrives in the course of time. Kaiser was his name." —HELEN KELLER

I had a client who welcomed a new puppy into his home within a few months of losing his elderly soul dog. He had to adjust to a new companion with a different temperament, much higher energy, and completely different needs. It was a lot to handle, especially while he was still grieving. He realized he was not ready yet, so the puppy is now living happily with a close family member alongside children and a big backyard. My client visits him often but, in his decision to give him a different home, he gave himself more time to grieve.

A new pet is not a "replacement" for the beloved animal companion you lost. They can never be replaced. Rather, a new pet allows for a different relationship and novel experiences. If you are not ready for this experience yet, or aren't sure if you'll ever be ready, that's okay. When—and if—you choose to welcome another pet into your home is a very personal decision.

I give myself all the time I need to decide what's best for me.

JANUARY 24

WHAT MADE YOUR PET SPECIAL? Write a journal entry describing your pet's special qualities. What tricks did they do? Did they win any competitions? How did they communicate with you? What were their most lovable or frustrating quirks? If they were a service animal, what services did they provide? What aspect of their personality meant the most to you?

I cherish you, departed friend.

JANUARY 25

“Animals are such agreeable friends—they ask no questions, they pass no criticism.” —GEORGE ELIOT

When a pet dies, any remaining animals in the home may also experience grief. The loss of a pet can affect the social hierarchy in the home and throw off daily routines. With consistent attention and enrichment, they will be okay. Try your best to stick to a consistent routine of sleep, exercise, and meals. Your love will buoy them (and theirs, you) in this time of transition in your home.

Grief is an experience shared by all beings who have known and lost love.

JANUARY 26

DO SOMETHING SPECIAL FOR THE GRIEVING ANIMALS IN YOUR HOME. (This applies to people, too.) Schedule time this week to give them extra care and attention. Provide them with their favorite treats. Play with them and their favorite toys. Spend extra time grooming them, if that's something they enjoy. Give them praise, love, and reassurance by speaking to them in a calm, gentle voice. The time you spend with them will provide comfort for them and healing for you.

I feel compassion for all beings who grieve.

JANUARY 27

"I bend, but do not break." —JEAN DE LA FONTAINE

Consider the willow tree: When hit with heavy storms, its branches bend and dance with the gusts to keep from snapping, while its roots hold the trunk steady. Grief often feels like a violent storm we won't be able to withstand. Remember that your grief comes from a place of boundless love for your pet. Allow yourself to be rooted by that love. Dancing with grief can strengthen your resilience. In your own way, and in your own time, you will process deep pain and trauma, heal, and then come back stronger. The trick is to lean in instead of resisting, so you can move with—and carefully through—the pain.

I can ride this storm by rooting myself firmly in love.

JANUARY 28

FRAME YOUR BELOVED PET WITH LOVE. Find a frame (maybe even heart shaped!) that will fit a favorite photo of your pet. This frame is a symbol of the way your love envelopes them now, and always. If you miss chatting with your pet, you can greet the photo in the morning or say good night to it at bedtime. You can talk to it about your workday, or wave to it on your way out. Don't worry, no one is judging you. Sometimes feeling a lost loved one a little closer is all our heart needs to feel calmer. If you don't feel comfortable doing that, take a minute to just smile at the sight of your sweet baby.

Our bond frames my life but knows no limits.

JANUARY 29

"I love talking about [grief], by the way, so if I cry it's only a beautiful thing. This is all the unexpressed love." —ANDREW GARFIELD

Some people avoid talking about their loss in certain situations. They worry they won't be able to control their emotional reaction. They fear they might burst into tears in the middle of work or in a public setting. But crying is a natural and expected part of the grieving process, even if you can't always control when and where it happens. It's helpful to let your tears flow if you're in a space where you feel safe doing so.

Tears are an expression of my love.

JANUARY 30

CREATE A GRIEVING SPACE IN YOUR HOME. Choose a spot in your home where you have privacy. Place a photo of your pet in this area and add a candle or whatever brings you comfort. Make sure you have a comfortable seating area. This week, pick a time when you'll have privacy. Light the candle, sit in your comfortable seat, and gaze at your pet's photo. You can talk to them about how you're feeling, write in your journal, call a friend, or simply be present in this peaceful space. Do whatever you think will open you up to your grief. Start with five minutes; let yourself stay longer if you need to.

I move forward according to my pace and needs.

JANUARY 31

"In all things it is better to hope than to despair."

—JOHANN WOLFGANG VON GOETHE

Grief can cause unexpected and sometimes overwhelming surges of emotion: sadness, guilt, anger—even despair. The truth is that while a part of you may always miss your beloved companion, the intensity of your pain will shift over time. Paradoxically, it's common to miss the sharpness of this pain once it subsides. You are experiencing a major change in your life, and it can be hard to adjust. You may need to actively seek hope and support as you move through this process.

Hope is within reach even from this place of grief.

FEBRUARY 1

CONSIDER ATTENDING A SUPPORT GROUP. Joining a pet grief support group can help you feel less alone. It might not be your thing at first, but many pet grievers report being surprised by how relieved they felt after sharing time and space with others experiencing similar loss. Their pain is active. You don't have to explain a thing. They may be in a different stage of grieving, and it could give you hope or solace to hear about what's helped them pull through. Most groups let you choose whether you want to share your story or to just listen. Speak to your veterinarian about any local in-person groups. If you prefer a virtual group, please see references in the back of this book.

I am not alone in my grief.

FEBRUARY 2

"No act of kindness, no matter how small, is ever wasted."

—AESOP

I had a client who was grieving the loss of her soul dog. She described her sweet pup as intuitively knowing when she was having a bad day. He would snuggle up next to her or do something playful that would bring a smile to her face. She shared, "He always wanted the best for me. He would want the best for me now." Whenever she was feeling especially down, it was knowing that he would want the best for her that motivated her to process her grief.

We humans extend kindness to our animal companions every day. We offer them love, food, and shelter. In return, they protect us, comfort us, entertain us, and even keep us active. What a gift it is to share our lives with animals! In times of intense grief, take a moment to focus on the purity of this reciprocal kindness that, as my client revealed, extends beyond life.

I find comfort in remembering the depth of your love.

FEBRUARY 3

CREATE A RÉSUMÉ FOR YOUR PET. How would you define their role in your life? Maybe they were the Entertainment Director, Cuddler in Chief, Chief Box Inspector, Bathroom Guardian, or Front Door Greeter. Create a list of the different roles they played in your life or write it up as a résumé.

I value all the roles you played in my life.

FEBRUARY 4

"Nothing is given so profusely as advice."

—FRANÇOIS VI, DUC DE LA ROCHEFOUCAULD

It's possible you will have a few awkward encounters throughout your grieving process. People may try to "fix" your problem. Others may ask you painful questions about your loss. Treat these moments as an opportunity to set compassionate boundaries for yourself. It's okay to thank people for their concern and politely end the conversation. Sometimes people just don't know what to say. It's okay to let them know what you do and do not need.

If I want advice, I can ask for it.

FEBRUARY 5

REHEARSE A FEW RESPONSES TO UNCOMFORTABLE QUESTIONS. Make a list of common questions and a few answers you feel comfortable saying. The day before you have an event or are going back to work, take a few minutes to practice your responses. If the person you are speaking with asks more uncomfortable questions, you can always gently tell them, "It's difficult to talk about this right now."

I can't control what people say to me, but I can choose how to respond.

FEBRUARY 6

"Waves of serener life pass over us from time to time, like flakes of sunlight over the fields in cloudy weather." —HENRY DAVID THOREAU

The nature of grief is wavelike. You may feel very sad for several days in a row, and then a little more hopeful. Right when you feel on the mend, sadness returns. A memory, an important day, or a location where you spent time together can trigger a wave of sorrow. Grief will ebb and flow, but over time you will learn ways to comfort yourself.

When I ride—rather than resist—the waves of grief, they become calmer and more manageable over time.

FEBRUARY 7

IF YOU ARE FEELING SAD, TRY THE "TOUCH" EXERCISE. Developed by Drs. Kristin Neff and Christopher Germer, the Mindful Self-Compassion approach teaches you to treat yourself as you would a loved one who is suffering. This exercise uses gentle and caring touch to express kindness to oneself. This week, whenever you feel a wave of sadness rise, offer yourself a soothing touch for 20 seconds. You can put one hand on your cheek, rest your right hand on your heart, or cross your arms and give yourself a gentle hug. If it feels safe to do so, close your eyes and take deep, calming breaths while you do this. If any of these gestures feel awkward or uncomfortable, you can try another gesture that feels right for you.

I practice compassion by being gentle with myself.

FEBRUARY 8

"People are changed by the experience [of bereavement]; they do not get over it, and part of the change is a transformed but continuing relationship with the deceased." —PHYLLIS R. SILVERMAN AND DENNIS KLASS

I have a client who keeps the remains of his beloved cat, Zooey, in a small urn, which he displays in his living room. In the first few weeks after his loss, he would place the urn right next to him on the nightstand. He said it gave him the feeling that Zooey was close by, as she was during their time together. He enjoyed the feeling of falling asleep imagining his kitty curled up and purring next to him. On special anniversaries, or when he especially misses her, he brings the urn into the bedroom, and it helps him fall asleep.

The bond you share with your beloved pet can be continued after they pass, either internally (e.g., imagining them with you) or externally (e.g., creating an altar or donating in their name). This model of grief is known as *continuing bonds*. By continuing the bond, your love lasts forever. Please note that everyone grieves differently, so if this model does not feel right to you, that's okay, too.

I cherish our bond in all its forms, for all time.

FEBRUARY 9

CREATE A GOOD-NIGHT RITUAL. Continue the bond with your beloved pet by making them part of your bedtime routine. Do only what feels comforting to you. Picture them in your mind and say "good night" before closing your eyes. Look at a photo of them and spend a few minutes telling them about your day. Consider placing something that belonged to them under your pillow, such as a piece of their blanket or their favorite toy.

I hold you in my heart.

APRIL 11

"You just have to honor them, love them, keep them alive in your mind." —GWYNETH PALTROW

Your memory of your animal companion can help you continue your bond with them. When you look at their photos, watch videos, or write about them, it strengthens your connection to them. You may even "feel them" by your side. Pleasure (or at least relief) can come in the very act of remembering. If you're not yet in a place to reminisce, choose one of the other distraction or mindfulness exercises in this book to help you cope.

Every act of remembering is a healing token of my love.

APRIL 12

MAKE A COLLAGE FROM PHOTOS OF YOUR PET. If you're moved to create a memento like a collage, collect photos of your pet to create a visual tribute. You can use printed photos or create your collage with digital tools. Don't worry about the "final product" or fret about whether it's "right" or aesthetically pleasing. Ultimately, what comes out of the process is much less important than engaging in the process itself.

Creation is a portal for remembrance and healing.

APRIL 13

"Tears and sorrows and losses are a part of what must be experienced in this present state of life." —LEIGH HUNT

Grieving an animal companion is different from grieving other losses. Their dependence on you was like that of a caregiver-child relationship. If your pet was a service animal, you are grieving the additional loss of the independence and support they provided. If they were a working animal, you are missing your partner, not just your pet. These losses are significant. It's okay if there are some days when you hardly cry and others where you sob frequently. It's your natural response to a devastating loss.

The weight of your absence is a sign of how full you made my life.

APRIL 14

REDUCE STRESS WITH THE 4-7-8 BREATHING TECHNIQUE. Try this breathing technique when you are feeling anxious or overwhelmed. Put one hand on your belly and notice how it rises on your inhale and falls as you exhale. Breathe in through your nose while counting to four. Hold your breath for seven counts. Exhale slowly through your mouth while counting to eight. Try this five to seven times to help you relax. This exercise can be particularly helpful at bedtime if you've been having trouble falling asleep.

I am powered by breath; I am soothed by breath.

APRIL 15

"Can't bring back time. Like holding water in your hand."

—JAMES JOYCE

Sometimes grief begins before a loss. Your pet may be elderly or diagnosed with a terminal illness. In trying to prepare yourself, it's like a piece of them has already left. This experience is known as *anticipatory grief*. You may experience the same strong emotions as the grief that follows a loss.

I had one client who took care of his ailing dog for several months. We worked on stress reduction to help him cope with caregiving, and cognitive behavior therapy to process his thoughts and feelings of anticipatory grief. After his dog passed, he shared that he felt comforted knowing that he had done everything possible to make his beloved companion feel safe and pain-free. Preparing for the loss emotionally—and committing to basic elements of his own self-care—helped him after his beloved pup was gone. If you are in the anticipatory grief stage, make sure to get plenty of rest and hydration and eat nutritious foods. Small steps make a big impact over time.

I can only care for others by first nourishing myself.

APRIL 16

HYDRATION AS SELF-CARE. Start every day this week with a refreshing glass of water. Your medical provider can tell you how many glasses of water per day is right for you. Consider filling a water bottle to carry on the go or keeping a pitcher of water in the fridge for ice-cold refreshment throughout the day. Note any changes you feel in your body.

Like water, I flow with life.

"There is no happiness like that of being loved by your fellow-creatures and feeling that your presence is an addition to their comfort."

—CHARLOTTE BRONTË

APRIL 17

Animal companions show genuine affection toward their humans. Take a moment to acknowledge the reciprocal nature of your affection. If your animal was a cuddler, the physical touch you shared was a two-way act of nurturing. They were relieved to get that special spot scratched, and you were soothed by the sensation of their fur in your hands. If they weren't cuddlers, maybe you had a bird who talked back to you or a horse who moved like an extension of your body once you hit the right stride.

This absence of mutual connection is one of the toughest aspects of pet loss. But there are ways to take small steps to ease this pain. Physical touch can have a calming effect on our nervous systems when we feel dysregulated. Consider creating something you can cuddle when you're needing the physical comfort that your animal companion brought (see April 18 for examples). Even if they weren't a cuddler, hugging their likeness can bring solace.

You expanded my ability to show and receive love in its purest form.

APRIL 18

CONSIDER CREATING A CUSTOM PILLOW MADE FROM YOUR PET'S IMAGE. You can print your animal's image on transfer paper, then iron it onto a cotton pillowcase. If you're not feeling crafty, there are online services that produce a variety of printed items with your photos. Alternatively, grabbing any (non-image) pillow will do. It might sound silly, but hugging a representation of your animal companion can bring a surprising amount of comfort.

This hurts. And still, I will keep on hugging and loving you.

APRIL 19

"Compassion is an emotion of which we ought never to be ashamed." —HUGH BLAIR

Compassionate people have sympathy for others in distress and are often motivated to alleviate their pain. Grieving after a loss increases your capacity for compassion. You know how it felt for you, but you also know that each person grieves differently. You wouldn't tell a grieving person how to grieve or how to feel. The most important thing is that you show them you are there for them. That's a power you've earned through the pain of this experience.

As I learn to be compassionate with myself, I learn to be compassionate with others.

APRIL 20

BE YOUR OWN BEST FRIEND TODAY. Practice self-compassion by reducing self-criticism and self-blame. Take a moment to identify any self-critical thoughts you've had in the last week. Include self-critical phrases that begin with, "I should have . . ." or "It's my fault that . . ." and write down what those thoughts are. Then, write what you would say to your best friend if they were in the same situation. Take a photo of your kind words. Every morning this week, look at this photo and read these compassionate words aloud to yourself. If you catch yourself saying something self-critical, replace it with your kind words.

My friendship extends to me.

APRIL 21

"Grief is a flower as delicate and prompt to fade as happiness." —MADAME DE GASPARIN

Brad first came to see me shortly after losing his cat Maddie. "I just can't stop crying." After we processed his loss together for a few sessions, he noted that "I still cry, but it's a lot less intense. I don't feel out of control, just sad." Gradually, Brad's grief began to fade, until a week before Maddie's birthday. Brad was worried, "I'm going to just fall apart on that day, there are too many memories."

I reassured him that this is a common response to significant days, and it doesn't mean that he's going backward. I helped Brad create an action plan to get through the day. The following week, Brad said, "Well, I didn't fall apart after all. I did cry because I missed her, but I know that's okay." He shared that he reached out to a caring friend, did one of the activities in his Tough Day Plan and "wished Maddie a happy, heavenly birthday."

Brad anticipated that his grief was going to spike on Maddie's birthday, but by creating a plan he was able to manage his emotions and experience a meaningful day.

I have everything I need to manage difficult days.

APRIL 22

MAKE A PLAN FOR TOUGH DAYS. Grief can be tough to manage on days that hold special meaning, such as your pet's "Gotcha Day," their birthday, or holidays. Prepare a plan to help you through it. Start by listing three activities you can do by yourself that you find comforting. Next, make a list of three people you can contact for support. Finally, list three simple tasks that give you a feeling of accomplishment. Take a photo of your plan or stick it somewhere that's easy to find.

I take care of myself by planning ahead.

APRIL 23

"All human wisdom is summed up in these two words, 'wait and hope.'" —ALEXANDRE DUMAS

Grief can't be rushed. Forcing yourself to "keep things moving" won't help. Take your time. If you feel overwhelmed by emotion, grounding exercises—like deep breathing, muscle relaxation, or focusing on each of your five senses—will help bring a sense of safety and reduce anxiety. In moments when even these feel challenging, simply place your feet (or any body part) flat on the floor. Focus on the ground and feel it. Notice the way you are connected to the earth. This will bring you into the present moment, and signal to your brain that you are safe.

No matter where I stand, the earth is beneath me. Supporting me. Constant.

APRIL 24

LEARN A GROUNDING EXERCISE. When you have a disturbing memory or are worrying about the future, a grounding exercise can help calm you by focusing your mind on the present. Let's try the 5-4-3-2-1 grounding exercise. Find a comfortable sitting or resting position. Take three deep breaths, inhaling through your nose and exhaling through your mouth. Look around you and name five things you see. Four things you can touch. Three things that you can hear. Two things you can smell. And finally, one thing you can taste. Finish with a couple of more deep breaths. (Modify this exercise in any way you like, such as skipping one of the senses or re-arranging the number of items.)

Awareness of my senses returns me to the present moment. I am alive!

APRIL 25

"To say that Josie was a member of our family doesn't even come close. She was my fur baby companion girl. She was my partner." —KERRY WASHINGTON, ABOUT HER LATE DOG, JOSIE

According to a 2023 Pew Research survey, 62 percent of US households have at least one pet, and 97 percent consider their pet a part of the family. This is why you will often hear caregivers refer to their animal companion as "my baby" or multiple animals in the family as brothers and sisters. When I speak to my nephews about my cat ReRe, I refer to her as their "cousin."

But numbers alone can't capture the profound role your pet played in your life. Maybe they were your quiet shadow, your steady comfort, your child's first best friend. They didn't just share your home; they shared your heart.

If you feel gutted by their absence, it's because your love was real and deep. And your grief will be, too. Let yourself feel the fullness of this loss. There is no need to minimize it, justify it, or compare it to anyone else's. This kind of love deserves to be mourned just as you see fit.

Our bond was real and profound, and so is my grief.

APRIL 26

IN WHAT WAYS WAS YOUR PET PART OF THE FAMILY? In your journal, describe how your pet was a part of your family. Write about what relationship your animal companion had with other members of the family, including the ones who didn't live with you. Write if they were spoiled by a grandparent or doted on by one of your siblings. Include any anecdotes about family activities. If you live by yourself, describe their quirks as a roommate.

You remain a part of my family, always.

APRIL 27

"We said goodbye to you this morning, Freddy . . . We will miss how you have to 'High Paw' us many times a day! . . . You lived so long that it doesn't feel right being in the house without you."

—HOLLY ROBINSON PEETE, ABOUT HER LATE DOG, FREDDY

Our pets are not just a member of our family; they also help make our living space a home. After losing a pet, it can be devastating to reorient our lives without them in it. We expect them to be there when we come home, bounding around the corner, or tucked in their favorite perch. If your pet lived on your property in a pen or a stall, the sense of emptiness is no different. It will take time to adjust to the new configuration of this emptiness, and the new meaning of home. Be kind to yourself as you make this transition.

I have the strength and inner resources to adjust to this difficult loss.

APRIL 28

FILL YOUR HOME WITH SOUND. If the new silence is too much, consider playing your favorite music, especially something that lifts your mood. If you prefer to have non-lyrical background sound, look for an ambient mix, such as the sounds of a café, gentle lo-fi beats, instrumentals, or classical music. Nature sounds such as ocean waves, summer rain, or a babbling brook are also soothing. If music isn't enough, turn on the TV (a comedy!) to hear the voice of others in another room.

As I learn to find solace in silence, I allow myself breaks with music and commotion.

APRIL 29

"Only people who are capable of loving strongly can also suffer great sorrow, but this same necessity of loving serves to counteract their grief, and heals them." —LEO TOLSTOY

Deciding whether to euthanize your pet or pursue another treatment is one of the most excruciating choices a guardian can face. There is no road map. You don't want your pet to suffer, but you also don't want to take away time with them that might still hold joy, comfort, or recovery. Intrusive thoughts creep in—*Did we give up too soon? Could we have waited longer?*

Even the most experienced veterinarians cannot predict outcomes with certainty. In the face of the unknown, it's important to remember that you chose love. You weighed the options from a place of deep compassion and care. You made the best decision you could with the knowledge and resources you had at the time. That is what love looks like: showing up, staying present, and making impossible decisions when your pet couldn't speak for themselves.

Now that you are grieving, second-guessing is a natural part of loss. But feeling guilty doesn't mean you did something wrong. It means your love was immense, and you're trying to make sense of something that hurts beyond words.

I release feelings of guilt and regret today.

APRIL 30

TAKE A QUIET MOMENT TO WRITE DOWN WHY YOU MADE THE DECISION YOU DID. List the ways you acted from love. Then, write the following sentence and complete it in your own words: *"If my pet could speak, I believe they would thank me for . . ."* Let this be a place of compassion, not judgment.

I made decisions from a place of love, not fear. My pet felt safe, cherished, and protected.

MAY 1

"My feeling is that there is nothing in life but refraining from hurting others and comforting those that are sad."

—OLIVE SCHREINER

Research suggests that a close bond with a pet nurtures empathy and compassion, and even provides the foundation for healthy friendships in children. According to the Society for the Prevention of Cruelty to Animals, kids who love animals tend to carry that care into how they treat others, too. So when a child loses a pet, the grief can be profound. It's likely not "just a pet" to them—it's a trusted companion, member of the family, and often their first experience with death.

There's no one way a child will express grief. Some may cry openly, while others retreat into silence, appear dismissive, or act out in confusion. Rather than rushing to explain or fix, offer a safe space for their experience to unfold. Gentle conversations, shared memories, or simply sitting together can all be acts of comfort. Even quiet gestures like drawing together, reading a children's book about pet loss, lighting a candle, or cuddling with a favorite toy can help a child feel seen, supported, and loved as they begin to make sense of their sorrow.

When I offer comfort with presence and love, I create a soft place for grief to land.

MAY 2

CREATE A MEMORY JAR. Create a jar full of different memories about your beloved animal companion. All you need is a large jar and note or origami paper. Gather everyone in the family including even the youngest child. Each person can write a few memories about your pet, fold it as they like, and place it in the jar. If you are using origami paper, consider folding the paper in the shape of a heart. If the little ones aren't old enough to write, they can dictate a memory to an adult or older child. Once the jar is filled, leave it somewhere accessible to everyone. Anytime someone feels sad and misses your animal companion, they can reach in the jar and pull out a memory to read. If you live alone, you can create a memory jar of your own, adding more memories at your own pace.

It's okay to remember. It's okay to feel. Love doesn't end.

MAY 3

"Honest, plain words best pierce the ear of grief."

—WILLIAM SHAKESPEARE

When you're grieving, you don't need to be "fixed." You need to grieve. It's supposed to be sad. It's supposed to hurt. You just need to know you are supported. If loved ones ask how they can help, let them know you want to hear something like: "I love you and care about you. I am here to listen when you want to talk or sit with you when you don't." If it feels right, you can let them know you'd appreciate help with groceries, running errands, or planning a memorial. Sometimes people need a reminder that simple words and kind gestures go a long way.

My heart is broken, but I am not broken. I will put the pieces back together over time.

MAY 4

GATHER A SMALL CIRCLE OF TRUSTED PEOPLE. Reach out to one or two people who you know can sit with you in silence or listen when you're ready to speak. Let them know ahead of time what you need; for example, "I'm not sure if I'm up to talking just yet, but it would mean a lot to me to just have you by my side." If vocalizing this need feels uncomfortable, you can write a short message, text, or letter to someone letting them know how they can help, even if it's just checking in to see how you're doing. Expressing your needs to others encourages connectedness and reduces isolation.

It is safe to let someone witness my sorrow.

MAY 5

"There is no grief which time does not lessen and soften."

—CICERO

If you work remotely, grieving the loss of a pet can be particularly challenging. Your pet was likely a constant companion throughout the day, and adjusting to the workspace without them can feel overwhelming. Colleagues who grew accustomed to seeing your pet during virtual meetings may ask about their absence, which can stir painful emotions. Over time, you will find it easier to respond to these questions, and they will gradually become less frequent. For now, lower the expectations you put on yourself. It's okay to need breaks, to step away, or to not have the perfect answer ready. Your sorrow doesn't need to be polished to be valid.

Seeing the reflection of my pet's absence is hard. It's okay that this is hard.

MAY 6

HOW TO MANAGE VIRTUAL MEETINGS WHEN YOU ARE GRIEVING. If your pet used to "participate" in meetings with you, it may feel odd to you to not have them nearby. To comfort yourself, hold one of their toys or a memory stone in your hands. If people reach out to you directly to ask how you are doing, consider typing up a couple of sentences that you can store in a notes program and copy-paste as an easy reply. Keep it simple and straightforward. You can let the person know if you are not ready to talk about it right now and thank them for their interest.

I can cope in any setting by keeping things simple.

"I don't like the work—no man does—but I like what is in the work—the chance to find yourself."

—JOSEPH CONRAD

MAY 7

Grief doesn't pause deadlines, responsibilities, or expectations. Whether your "work" means a job, caregiving, creative pursuits, or daily survival, it may feel impossibly heavy right now—or strangely comforting. Some find solace in routine; others need space to step away. There is no "right" way.

Some symptoms of grief, such as irritability and difficulty concentrating, impact productivity and social engagement. What matters is honoring your limits while being gentle with yourself. You may find that showing up to your work helps you stay grounded, or you may need to pull back. Either way, your grief is valid, even if no one sees the depth of your pain.

I create a work/life balance in my life, even in difficult times.

MAY 8

MAKE A PLAN FOR TAKING TIME OFF, IF YOU NEED IT. If you're self-employed or run your own business, consider delegating tasks or canceling clients for at least a week. This *is* a family emergency—and most people will understand. If you have commitments you can't miss, try to cancel non-essential meetings or responsibilities to create some breathing room.

If you work for someone else, check your employee handbook or company website. While most workplaces don't offer formal pet bereavement leave, you may be able to use sick days, PTO, or vacation time. You can also talk with HR or your employee assistance program. You don't have to explain the details—simply say you're experiencing significant personal stress and need time to step back.

It is okay to press pause.

MAY 9

"To exist is to change, to change is to mature, to mature is to go on creating oneself endlessly." —HENRI-LOUIS BERGSON

For many, being a pet parent is more than a role; it's a piece of who they are. One of my clients, Adam, described feeling invisible after he lost his beloved dog Chicky—they went everywhere together. Chicky had her circuit in the neighborhood, pinpointing the stores and cafés with the best treats. Everyone greeted Adam as "Chicky's dad." When Chicky died, he avoided their old circuit for weeks. The thought of sharing the news was just too painful. Who was he to these people if not "Chicky's dad"?

Eventually, as Adam's grief began to fade, he started going to a few of Chicky's old haunts. As he expected, everyone from the barista at his favorite coffeeshop to the attendant at the dry cleaners asked, "Where's Chicky?" Adam shared he was touched by how much people cared not only about Chicky, but also, to his surprise, Chicky's dad. Everyone offered condolences and comfort. Adam said he realized that while his community had deep fondness for Chicky, *he* was also a valued member. He was the one, after all, who showed up every day, struck up conversation, and supported local businesses.

When your animal is gone, it can feel like part of your identity disappears with it. Let yourself acknowledge that shift without needing to define who you are next. You are still you, just tender, changed, and becoming. Let this unfolding happen in its own time.

As I change, I carry forward the love that shaped me.

MAY 10

WHAT IDENTITY DID CAREGIVING PROVIDE FOR YOU? Write about how you saw yourself in relationship to your pet. Describe how you think you were seen in your community or by your family and friends. Identify one to two ways you can maintain aspects of this identity, such as supporting animal organizations. Widening the scope, jot down one to two additional qualities you admire in yourself, independent from any aspect of caregiving.

While I care for others, my worth extends beyond caretaking.

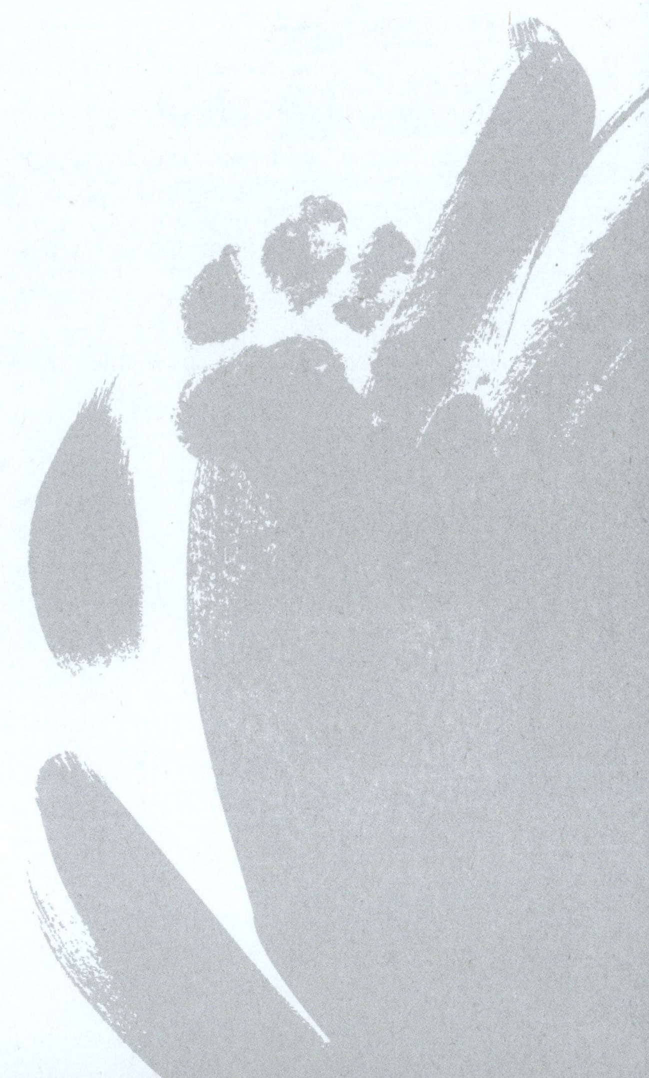

MAY 11

"I have cried too many tears to count—the type of tears that make you get in the shower with the absurd hope that the running water on your face will somehow make you not feel them, or pretend they're not there. But they are. And that's okay too." —MEGHAN MARKLE

Sometimes we experience more than one loss in a short period of time. You may find you are uncharacteristically upset about the loss of a distant relative or death of an acquaintance if these events coincide with the loss of your pet. That's because each time you experience a loss, it opens old wounds. This is known as *compounded grief*—when one loss reactivates the pain of earlier ones, creating a swirl of emotions that feel larger than the moment at hand.

Compounded grief can feel overwhelming, confusing, or "bigger than it should be," but that doesn't mean you're grieving "wrong." It means you are carrying more than one loss at once. Healing may take more time and care, and that's okay. Let your tears flow, trusting they are evidence of how deeply you've cared, across time.

I allow myself to grieve without shame, without rushing.

MAY 12

CREATE A RECENT LOSS INVENTORY. Grief can stir memories of past losses, some you've grieved, and others held quietly inside. When you're ready, take a few moments to reflect on the past few years. Were there any significant losses? This might include the death of another pet, the passing of a loved one, the end of a relationship, a move, a lost job, or even a fading friendship.

Name the emotions that you feel when you think of each loss. Allow yourself to just sit with them for a few moments. Resist the urge to analyze or solve; you're here to witness and honor your experience. Now imagine wrapping each loss in a soft cloth, giving it space, but not letting it take over. This is how we practice tending to grief without being consumed by it. Complete this activity by doing something soothing like sipping warm tea or taking a walk.

I've overcome obstacles in the past. I draw strength from these experiences as I apply them to my sorrow today.

MAY 13

"If I can stop one Heart from breaking, I shall not live in vain."

—EMILY DICKINSON

Grief is often accompanied by stress, and when extreme stress floods your body with hormones, it can cause inflammation and pain and lower your resistance to infection. In other words, grief hurts—literally. If you already suffer from chronic pain, you might feel your pain more intensely than usual. You might also experience insomnia or poor diet, both of which negatively impact health. That's why it is especially important to do your best to take care of your health while you are grieving.

I do my best to nurture my body. When my body speaks, I listen.

MAY 14

START THE DAY WITH GENTLE STRETCHING. Stretching in the morning can help wake up your body, improve circulation, and release tension that may have built up overnight. It can also support emotional well-being by grounding you in your body before the day begins. Even a few minutes of movement—like slow shoulder rolls, neck stretches, or gentle side bends—can ease stiffness and help you feel more centered as you face the day.

With gentle movement, I create space for renewal.

MAY 15

"Something I tell myself: Take it easy. Every day is an opportunity to reevaluate and shift habits, to connect, to mend, to look for flow. It'll be ok." —JENNIFER GARNER

Caring for a pet helps us organize our lives. We have regular routines related to their care: getting out of bed to feed them, taking a walk or visiting the park, going on weekly trips to the pet store—the list goes on. One of the most excruciating parts of pet loss is the abrupt disruption to these routines. This shift can make the day feel longer and throw off our own daily rhythm.

While you are working through your grief, it's helpful to establish a daily routine for yourself. This will keep you healthy and reduce stress. The key is to start small. Choose one anchor point in your day—like morning coffee or an evening walk—and gently build around it. There's no need to develop a full-fledged schedule. Let your new rhythm take shape slowly, as you listen to what your body, mind, and spirit need.

With time, life will regain its rhythm.

MAY 16

ADD ONE NEW THING TO YOUR MORNING ROUTINE. Knowing what to expect in those early hours of the morning can support you as you move through waves of grief. A regular morning routine can also boost your overall mood and focus throughout the day. If you don't have one, try picking two to three from the list below to get you started.

- ❑ Get out of bed within five minutes of waking up
- ❑ Make your bed
- ❑ Open the drapes/curtains
- ❑ Drink a cold glass of water
- ❑ Brush your teeth
- ❑ Take a shower
- ❑ Wash your face
- ❑ Moisturize
- ❑ Stretch, meditate, or do yoga
- ❑ Make tea or coffee
- ❑ Eat breakfast

I start my day by putting myself first.

MAY 17

"The knowledge that we cannot hold on forever to those we love makes us hold them all the more dearly." —H. A. OVERSTREET

Taking care of a pet in their final months means taking on the tasks of chef, nurse, and chauffeur—as well as watching their behavior closely to make sure they continue to enjoy a good quality of life. While love drives this care, it can feel taxing, and their loss might bring a sense of relief. This is a natural reaction to the stress of caregiving. It does not mean that you are glad your pet is gone or that you are selfish. Remind yourself how much you did for your beloved, and that it's okay to exhale now.

I am allowed to feel relieved that the hardest part is behind us. I extend compassion to myself as I make sense of complicated feelings.

MAY 18

TAKE CARE OF YOUR HEALTH BY SCHEDULING A CHECKUP. You may have been so busy taking care of your pet that your own health took a back seat. Make a list of any overdue visits, such as annual physicals, screenings, or dental cleanings. This week, pick a different appointment to schedule each day. If you're already up-to-date, honor yourself by planning something that supports your well-being, whether it's a walk in nature, a nourishing meal, or a quiet moment of rest.

My well-being matters. I deserve the same care and attention I so lovingly gave to my pet.

MAY 19

"Exercise is really important to me—it's therapeutic."

—MICHELLE OBAMA

When you're grieving, even the smallest tasks can feel overwhelming—so finding the motivation to exercise might seem especially hard. But movement, even in its simplest forms, can be a powerful tool for healing. Exercise has a positive impact on your mental and physical well-being during the grieving process because movement helps release difficult emotions (think kickboxing if you're feeling angry or frustrated) and reduces stress. It's also one of the most effective ways to regulate the nervous system when you're feeling emotionally or mentally overwhelmed. If you're struggling with sleep, physical activity helps tire your body enough to invite more restful sleep. No matter your age or mobility level, there's an option that can work for you.

Each day, I discover more and more of my inner—and outer—strength.

MAY 20

DEDICATE TIME TO MOVE YOUR BODY. Find a day this week to move your body for at least 20 minutes. Empower yourself to start small—a short walk or gentle stretches can be highly beneficial. The goal is to increase your heart rate and sustain this for even a short period of time. If you haven't exercised in a while—or ever—speak to a doctor or physical therapist about how to get started. In addition to improving cardiovascular, brain, and immune health, this type of activity can unlock some of the stickier aspects of grief. If you and your pet exercised together, it's okay to take a break from those activities and give yourself time as you reintroduce movement into your life.

My body knows how to move, release, and renew.

MAY 21

“Mute grief feels a keener pang than that which cries aloud.”

—PUBLILIUS SYRUS

No matter how prepared you think you are for the loss of your pet, your reaction to it may surprise you. Sometimes in your pet's final days, you are so busy trying to keep them comfortable and preparing for your loss that you may be on autopilot. After they are gone, you may be overwhelmed with emotions that haven't had a chance to surface, such as anger and despair. Your mind may try to protect you from the shock of the loss, making you feel numb or as if time has slowed down. Be gentle with yourself as you get to know the contours of your grief.

I will allow my grief to take the shape and form it needs to take for me to process it.

MAY 22

DE-STRESS WITH GUIDED IMAGERY. Find a quiet place to sit. Close your eyes if you feel safe doing so, and let your body relax. Imagine you are somewhere that's calm and safe. It could be a place from the past, the present, or an imaginary location. Use all your senses to imagine the sights and sounds around you. Let the tranquility of this place wash over you. Slowly repeat grounding statements like “I am safe” and “I am calm.”

I still feel the love of my pet with me. I am safe. Our bond of love continues.

MAY 23

"She did not want to talk of her sorrow, but with that sorrow in her heart she could not talk of outside matters." —LEO TOLSTOY

Talking about your feelings after the loss of your animal companion can be an effective way to process grief. But it can be upsetting to have to repeatedly answer questions about their passing, especially if it was due to an unexpected illness or accident. You are not obliged to provide a detailed explanation. It's okay to keep your story to yourself as this loss settles in your heart.

Our story is a precious gem that I hold in the palm of my hand, mine to keep or give.

MAY 24

REHEARSE A SIMPLE EXPLANATION ABOUT YOUR LOSS. Practicing a simple answer of just a few sentences will make it easier to respond, especially if you're caught off guard. For example, "Yes, Joni passed away on Tuesday. I really am going to miss her. I don't feel like talking about the details right now." If you're ready to share memories, you can say something like, "You know what I'm really going to miss?" or better yet, ask them to share a memory of your pet with you. Of course, words may not be the answer right now. Set your boundaries as firmly as you need to as you move through your own healing process.

I draw the boundaries in my grieving process and in all matters of my body, mind, and heart.

MAY 25

"Look within; within is the fountain of all good."

—MARCUS AURELIUS

You opened your heart and home to your beloved pet, but you may not be ready to care for a new companion animal. It's likely, though, that helping animals is an important value to you. According to Dr. Steven Hayes, who developed acceptance and commitment therapy (ACT), aligning your actions with your values increases well-being and helps build a sense of purpose. Finding ways to make life better for animals, even indirectly, can help you find comfort while you are grieving.

You taught me the beauty of caring for others.

MAY 26

THINK ABOUT THE MANY WAYS YOU CAN HELP ANIMALS. If you are not ready to interact with animals, there are still many things you can do to help them. You can organize or join a cleanup day at a forest preserve, park, or beach. Closer to home, you can provide seeds for birds and water for other critters. You can plant native pollinator and bird-friendly plants. You can also go to the library or look online to read about protecting oceans and forests. If you live near a migratory bird flight path, consider making your windows bird-safe with reflective tape, string, film, and stickers.

I allow my kind and caring heart to gently guide me as I continually evolve and find my purpose.

MAY 27

"RIP to our amazing goldfish we loved so much. 14 YEARS!!!!!!!!" —LAURA DERN

Society often doesn't offer the same level of sympathy for pet loss as it does for the loss of a human loved one. It can be even harder to find acceptance and social support, so helpful when grieving, if you have a pet other than a cat or dog. It's important to know that you are not alone.

There are millions of devoted caregivers to fish, reptiles, birds, and small mammals. Others care for fowl, pot-bellied pigs, horses, and even rescued marine animals. You cared for and loved your pet and deserve sympathy and support as much as anyone grieving a loss.

The quality of my love is not diminished by the judgments or assumptions of others who do not understand. Our love deserves honor and respect.

MAY 28

THINK OF ADVICE YOU'D GIVE TO SOMEONE CARING FOR A PET OF THE SAME SPECIES OR BREED AS YOURS. You have learned a lot about caring for your pet. Each species requires a different diet, types of enrichment, and habitat. What are some of the most helpful tricks and tips you could share with a new caregiver? Consider joining an online group devoted to your species to share your tips.

I will always be someone with a deep love for animals. I have much to offer the world around me, should I choose to share.

MAY 29

"Wrinkles should merely indicate where smiles have been."

—MARK TWAIN

Losing a pet can be particularly difficult for anyone living alone, especially seniors who may also be retired or grieving multiple losses (those of friends, loved ones, or aspects of their health) or those facing their own terminal diagnosis. Pets provide company and structure for us all; the loss of these comforts can be particularly devastating in later or fragile stages of life. If part of your pain is around this being your "last pet," allow yourself time to grieve both the loss of this pet and what this means for you as a pet caregiver.

This shift in identity can also stir questions in you around purpose. It's important to remind yourself that you still can identify as someone who loves and cares for animals. You can find comfort in remembering the many ways you have helped the animals you've cared for. In the meantime, find solace by engaging in comforting activities that remind you of your worth, right here in this moment.

Our years today are a bright spot in my life. I cherish them now and always.

MAY 30

TEND TO THE GREEN ELEMENTS OF LIFE. Spending time with plants—whether in a garden, on a balcony, or by a windowsill—can be quietly healing. Watering, weeding, or planting something new invites you into the rhythm of life continuing, even amid grief. If you don't have a garden, consider caring for an indoor plant. You can visit a local nursery to ask for a low-maintenance one to start with. You don't need a green thumb, just a small act of care. Watching something grow, even slowly, can be a gentle reminder that your love still has somewhere to go.

As I care for this living thing, I witness my love in action.

MAY 31

"Give this one day to thanks, to joy, to gratitude."

—HENRY WARD BEECHER

There may have been other people who contributed to the everyday well-being of your pet. This could be inside or outside your home: partners, kids, relatives—dog walkers, pet-sitters, groomers, and vets. Neighbors and friends might have also helped care for your pet in ways big and small. Taking a moment to honor the time and energy these people invested in your pet's well-being may lift their spirits, and yours.

The community we built is still around me.

JUNE 1

EXPRESS GRATITUDE TO THE PEOPLE WHO HELPED CARE FOR YOUR PET. This week, consider sending one or two thank-you cards or emails to anyone who improved the quality of your pet's life. That gratitude could extend to staff at the pet-supply store who gave you helpful advice, or the delivery person who gave your pet a treat every time they dropped off a package. Letting people know how much they meant to your pet's well-being is an actionable way for you to memorialize your pet.

I am grateful for the kindness of those who loved and cared for my pet. Their support lives in my heart alongside the love I carry forward.

JUNE 2

"How beautiful a day can be
When kindness touches it!" —GEORGE ELLISTON

When we care for animals we practice a quiet, daily form of kindness—filling food bowls, offering comfort, showing up again and again with love. Our pets feel that care deeply, even if they never say the words. And we feel it, too, in return: the head resting on a lap, the tail wag, the soft nudge of a nose.

After a loss, the absence of these small exchanges can feel overwhelming. That steady rhythm of giving and receiving is suddenly gone. But the kindness you offered did not disappear. It lives on in your memories, in your heart, and in the lasting imprint of your bond. You don't have to decide now whether or how to offer that love again. But know that your capacity for kindness remains—at your own pace, in your own way.

I think of you as I extend kindness to others.

JUNE 3

MAKE A LIST OF VOLUNTEER OPPORTUNITIES TO HELP ANIMALS.
There are many ways to help animals lead better lives. If it feels right, this week, spend some time exploring potential volunteering options. This may include working a shift at a shelter, fundraising for an animal welfare organization, supporting conservation efforts, or asking a neighbor if they need support while on vacation. Shelters need photographers to take pictures of adoptable pets, and writers to create their bios. You don't have to start volunteering now (or ever). But if and when you feel ready, these resources will be waiting for you.

As I offer kindness to animals in need, I feel the legacy of my pet living on through me.

JUNE 4

"One thing about fires: they happen fast . . . Heartbreakingly, we lost all four of our pets. We are still sitting with that loss, but we are lucky we got to love them at all."

—CATERINA SCORSONE

Losing a pet due to an accident or natural disaster can cause a type of grief called *traumatic grief*. With traumatic grief, it's natural to feel angry toward anyone associated with the event, or guilty because you believe you could have prevented the accident from happening.

This happened to my client Ben who was heartbroken by the loss of his beloved cat, Sally, due to a house fire. Ben blamed himself because he was not at home when the fire started, and by the time he rushed home it was too late. Ben had developed symptoms of PTSD, so I engaged him in cognitive processing therapy (CPT). Ben identified his beliefs about the traumatic event and, one by one, slowly began to question them. He realized he was so focused on blaming himself that he had ignored important facts about the fire, such as the report from the fire department showing the fire was caused by faulty equipment and had spread rapidly. Ben said, "You know, the fire was actually *not* my fault at all. I wish it didn't happen, but there was no way I could have prevented it." In reexamining the stories he was telling himself, he was able to attend to his mourning and process his grief.

Note: If you think you might be experiencing post-traumatic stress disorder (PTSD), please see the resources in the back of the book for more comprehensive support. It's an act of bravery to ask for help.

I trust that anger is a normal reaction to tragedy and grief. I release any self-blame that weighs me down.

JUNE 5

TRY GROUNDING STATEMENTS. When you are having repetitive thoughts or traumatic memories, grounding yourself in the present moment can help reduce your stress response. This is a way of letting your brain know that the traumatic event is not currently happening, and that you are safe where you are. Try a statement that includes who you are, what date and time it is, and where you are. Then add the words, "I am safe." For example, "My name is Sandra, today is Friday, May 21. It is noon, and I am in my living room at home. I am safe." The next time you are feeling overwhelmed, take a few deep breaths and then slowly say the grounding statement. Repeat this at least three times.

I am grounded in the present moment.

JUNE 6

"The ocean has its ebbings, so has grief."

—THOMAS CAMPBELL

Grief comes in waves. You may go several weeks or months without it impacting your life, and then something random will trigger a memory and you're suddenly drowning in it again. You might feel the instinct to escape. You were starting to feel better—why are these horrible emotions back? The problem is that difficult emotions can sometimes act like a riptide: The more you try to swim against its pull, the harder it pulls you in, and the farther from shore you get. The trick to getting out of the riptide isn't to swim against the current—it's to swim parallel to the shore so you can get away from the undercurrent. In this same way, the best way through those moments of grief isn't going against it, but alongside it.

I flow with the waves, not against them.

JUNE 7

MINDFULLY ACKNOWLEDGE YOUR GRIEF. This week, when you experience a spike in grief, try this mindfulness technique. First, acknowledge your grief verbally without judgment. For example, "I'm grieving now. It's my natural response to the loss I've experienced." Name the emotions you are experiencing, starting with the words, "I feel . . ." Identify where you feel the grief in your body. It might be an empty feeling in the pit of your stomach, or tension in your neck or shoulders. Take a deep breath and when you exhale, imagine your breath relaxing the part of your body where grief hurts the most. Complete this exercise with a comforting activity, like sipping a warm beverage or listening to a relaxing song.

I gently acknowledge whatever phase of grief I am in right now. I honor this place, knowing I will not be here forever.

JUNE 8

"I know two things for sure: Norbert made this world a better place, and his spirit will live on through our smiles in his community, the Norberthood." —JULIE STEINES, MOM OF POPULAR INTERNET THERAPY DOG, NORBERT

Animals have become influencers in their own right. There are cats, dogs, birds, rabbits, tortoises, foxes (and more!) with millions of online followers who watch them do funny, mischievous, or therapeutic things. Viewers may feel like they know these animals, even grieving them when they pass. While you are grieving the loss of your pet, the loss of another animal in your circle, whether in-person or virtual, may trigger unresolved feelings around your late pet. This is normal. Give yourself time to process these tangential emotions without shame.

Every emotion is a natural response. There is no shame in nature.

JUNE 9

TAKE A NATURE BREAK. Brainwave studies suggest that nature can have a calming effect on our nervous systems. If you are not near a natural setting, have mobility issues, or the weather is not cooperating, you can still take a trip outside. Research indicates that watching videos and simulated nature content can also have a restorative effect. Picking up a travel magazine or spending 10 minutes enjoying the natural wonders from Instagram accounts such as @earth, @nature_org, and @natgeotravel will likely calm and transport you.

I allow myself breaks to connect to the beauty of this earth.

JUNE 10

"RIP, [Buddy], I will love you forever and never forget you."

—DEMI LOVATO, ABOUT HER LATE PUPPY, BUDDY

In the weeks and months after a loss, painful memories of your pet during their last days may stand out more vividly. Allow yourself to access memories of when they were healthy and happy, too. If you're struggling with lingering doubts or regrets, writing your thoughts down or speaking with someone you trust can help you move toward a more compassionate, forgiving perspective. As Demi Lovato notes in the quote above, our love for our beloved animal companions is eternal.

Everything I did for you, until the end, was guided by love.

JUNE 11

REMEMBER YOUR PET AT THEIR HEALTHIEST. If you're ready, choose a photo where your pet is thriving. They can be running, playing, or simply lounging around. If they had chronic health issues or you adopted them as a senior, it could be a moment where they look at ease. Take a few minutes to write a description of the moment. Use all your senses to re-create it. How do you know they were happy here? How did you help them feel their best? If you aren't yet ready to look at photos, just take a moment to think about a time when you knew your pet was content.

I gave my pet a life filled with love, safety, and joy. Their happiest moments reflect the care we shared.

JUNE 12

"Alone we can do so little, together we can do so much." —HELEN KELLER

What a delight it is to walk into a business and find a pet in charge. There are "working pets" in many stores and offices greeting customers, boosting worker morale, managing security, and performing pest control. If you are grieving the loss of a working pet you cared for, it may be difficult for you to go back to work at first. It's likely, though, that you will be sharing your loss with coworkers and customers. Regardless of the animal companion you are grieving, togetherness can be a bridge from the depths of sorrow to shared love and eventually, hope.

There can be solace in shared spaces. I trust in support of my chosen community.

JUNE 13

BRING A TREAT OR TOY TO A WORKING PET IN YOUR TOWN. If you know of any store or job site in your town that has a pet on staff, consider stopping by with a toy or treat for them. You can also call your local police K9 unit—or find out if the town firehouse has a pet—and ask if they will accept a donation. The gesture has the possibility of bringing joy to the working pet, its humans, and you.

When I take action in your name, I feel connected to you.

JUNE 14

"[Gabbana] was more than a pet. She was my first child, my companion and my friend . . . I never thought I would be this devastated over [losing] a dog but 14 years, is a long time together." —KHLOÉ KARDASHIAN

If your pet was with you for many years, you have likely endured the full spectrum of life together—the highest highs and lowest lows. Time deepened the bond to a level where they felt inextricable from your life. In short: It's not easy to adjust to life without their physical presence. Your brain still expects them to be there, even though you "know" they won't be. It can be helpful to change routines or engage in new activities so their absence is not as jarring. Shifting activities can help shift your perspective.

I trust the evolution of my grief.

JUNE 15

CREATE A TIMELINE OF EVENTS YOU'VE SHARED WITH YOUR PET. These can be personal milestones as well as historical events. Start by jotting down the date you welcomed your pet into your life. Put your date of birth if your pet was already part of your family when you were born. Then write down five important events that have happened in your life between then and now. Describe what was going on in your life at the time, and how your pet interacted with you. Did they keep you company during the COVID-19 pandemic? Did they celebrate with you when your favorite team won a championship? Remembering how much you shared will help you maintain a sense of connection and meaning.

When I think of you, we are connected.

JUNE 16

"The thing is to find a truth which is true for me."

—SØREN KIERKEGAARD

For many people, spirituality can be of great comfort following the loss of a beloved pet. It is very common for people to think about concepts such as the soul and reincarnation. Many wonder if they will see their beloved animal again in some form or receive a sign from them. There are many different beliefs about the afterlife unique to each religion and culture that you can explore. People who don't follow a religion may find exploring philosophical writings and cultural traditions helpful instead.

If I need to, I can seek comfort and guidance in forces greater than myself.

JUNE 17

EXPLORE BELIEFS ABOUT ANIMALS AND SPIRITUALITY. Start by exploring your own religious and cultural traditions. You can speak to elders in your community or a spiritual advisor. Do an online search or visit a library to explore other beliefs about animals and the afterlife. If you have no interest in religious beliefs, consider exploring how philosophers throughout the ages and from different cultures viewed the human-animal bond.

I embrace my spirituality in whatever form is true for me.

JUNE 18

"There is indeed both need to talk about one's loss and to avoid talking about it, to accept and deny the reality of the death. Laughter may mingle with sorrow, relief with regret." —MARGARET STROEBE

In the 1990s, prominent Dutch psychologists Margaret Stroebe and Henk Schut developed the dual process model of coping with bereavement. The model describes grief as two oscillating processes. One is loss-oriented—actively focusing on loss by processing emotions and engaging in rituals. The other is restoration-oriented—adapting to changes in your life, developing new routines, and exploring new relationships and activities. In your day-to-day life, you go back and forth between the two processes. This allows you to begin rebuilding your life while also allowing enough time for you to grieve your loss.

I can process the pain of loss in small doses, and in the pauses restore my well-being.

JUNE 19

PRACTICE THE DUALITY OF GRIEF. This morning, allow 30 minutes to focus on your grief. This can include writing in a journal, going through items in your memory box, or spending time in a grief corner in your home. Later in the day, spend 30 minutes focusing on restoration. Spend time engaging in a new activity you've been wanting to try, or something you haven't done in a while. Feel free to adjust this exercise in a way that fits your schedule—the idea is to find a balance between grieving and healing as you move through the day.

I can move freely back and forth between attending to my life and attending to my grief.

JUNE 20

"The next best thing to the enjoyment of a good time, is the recollection of it." —JAMES LENDALL BASFORD

Because pets are family, we often celebrate holidays and other events with them. We include them in family holiday photos and greeting cards. We dress them for parties or events—their costumes can be the most fun part of Halloween! Pets might receive special gifts, treats, or meals in accordance with holiday tradition (or sneak food from the holiday table). You may experience a resurgence of your grief symptoms on holidays, even years after the loss of your pet. Talking about how you involved your pet in holidays, and finding ways to include their memory in your new and existing holiday traditions will help you manage these sticky days.

I find comfort in setting aside special moments just for you.

JUNE 21

CREATE A HOLIDAY MEMORIES SLIDESHOW, COLLAGE, OR STORY. Find photos of your pet on different holidays throughout the years. Combine them digitally or, if you're feeling crafty, print out photos for a paper collage. If it's still too painful to look through photos, consider writing a brief story or simply remembering a favorite holiday spent with your pet.

I celebrate the memories of holidays with you.

JUNE 22

"Patience is a remedy for every sorrow." —PUBLILIUS SYRUS

Many people who are grieving find that reminiscing about their pet helps them feel closer to them and provides comfort. And yet, it may take time to be able to reminisce without feeling overwhelmed by emotion. One way to ease this process is to start by talking about your pet and then work your way up to looking at pictures or videos. Everyone grieves differently, so there are no rules or "normal" here. Be patient with yourself and go at your own pace. During this process, it is okay to take a break with a healthy distraction if you need some reprieve.

I trust the trajectory of my grief. Each day, I feel the memories of you become more pleasant.

JUNE 23

MAKE TIME FOR FUN AND GAMES. Grieving can be exhausting. While it's important for you to explore and express your emotions, game playing can be a supportive part of the healing process. The focus required to play a game (any game!) can pull you away from ruminating about your loss. If you prefer in-person games, invite a friend or family member to play a game with you, or schedule a casual game night. There are plenty of games to play on your phone. If you like playing computer or console games, set a timer for an hour and have at it! If you prefer solitary games, enjoy a crossword or Sudoku puzzle. The important thing is to engage in a healthy distraction from grief.

There is a role for "fun and games" even in the darkest of times.

JUNE 24

"I wish I had no heart, it aches so . . ." —LOUISA MAY ALCOTT

If you choose to cremate your pet, retrieving the remains can be one of the most difficult moments in the mourning process. Holding that box in your hands makes the loss feel very real. You can prepare in advance by speaking to your vet or euthanasia provider about the logistics of this process.

Of course, there is the question of what to do with the remains once they're in your possession. One of my clients had a beloved cat named Mimi. He kept Mimi's cremains in a beautiful urn on a shelf in his living room. But when he had to leave for a three-week work trip, he could not bear the thought of leaving Mimi all alone in his apartment. So he brought the urn to his sister's house. "I felt comforted by the thought that Mimi would be cared for while I was away," he shared. As in all areas of grief, if something feels right to you, it probably is.

I will continue to care for you by caring for and honoring your memory.

JUNE 25

HONOR YOUR PET'S CREMATED REMAINS. Finding meaningful ways to honor your pet's memory can be a comforting part of the grieving process. If you choose cremation, you might use small portions of the cremains for different tributes. Be sure to check local laws first, then consider gently scattering the ashes in a place your pet loved. Some people find comfort in keeping the cremains in an urn displayed in a special room, perhaps where you and your pet spent time together—as a way to feel their presence close by. There are also online services that create keepsakes, such as pendants or rings, from the cremains.

I honor your memory in a way that's unique to my heart.

JUNE 26

"The heart has always the pardoning-power."

—MADAME SWETCHINE

Grieving a pet who died in a natural disaster is often accompanied by guilt. Remember you had to make quick decisions while being terrified and in an unpredictable environment. You may have been away from your home during a sudden event, like a tornado or earthquake. If you were at home, you may not have been able to get everyone to safety in time. You may have decided to shelter in place because the shelters near you did not accept animals. Finally, you might be dealing with PTSD from the trauma of the event itself, in addition to grieving the loss of your pet. Be compassionate with yourself as you gently work through these layers of grief.

I recognize there is much beyond my control. Each action I made in crisis was rooted in deep love and care for those around me.

JUNE 27

CREATE A SMALL, PORTABLE MEMORIAL SPACE. If you're displaced, navigating the uncertainty after a natural disaster, or otherwise feeling "lost," consider creating a small, portable tribute to your pet—something simple like a photo, a collar, or a favorite toy in a small bag or box. You can carry it with you, set it by your bedside, or place it somewhere meaningful. Rituals like these can offer a sense of grounding and connection while honoring your pet amid the chaos. Later, you may choose to expand on this tribute, but for now, it's okay to keep it simple and personal.

As I sift through each layer of grief, I find ways to keep you with me.

JUNE 28

"Death is hard to understand, maybe even harder to accept." —LUPITA NYONG'O

Love for your pet was, quite literally, hardwired in your brain. Routines, caring for them, and physically bonding created pathways in your brain that linked you together. That's why when you wake up in the morning, your first instinct is to get up to feed them. When you come home after being away for the day, you expect them to greet you as you walk in. This untangling is a natural, and sometimes heartbreaking, part of the pet grieving process. Be patient with yourself as your brain plays catchup. And take solace in the fact that while daily actions might change, special memories are forever etched in your mind.

Our love is hardwired in my brain.

JUNE 29

START YOUR DAY BY TALKING TO YOUR PET. Talking out loud to your pet is a normal, healthy way to develop a connection to them after they're gone. You can think of it as speaking to the loving memory of them that you now hold in your heart. This week, try saying a pleasant good morning to them. Make sure to include their name or nickname in your greeting. Look at a picture of them or imagine them in your mind as you speak to them. It's okay to add "I love you" or "I miss you." As with all activities in this book, if this doesn't resonate with you, feel free to skip or adapt it to your preference.

I start each day with love for you.

JUNE 30

"Can this world, From of old, Always have been so sad, or did it become so for the sake, of me alone?" —ANONYMOUS

There may be days when you don't feel like getting out of bed. The pain and sadness of grief has drained your energy. You think of undone tasks and say, "I'll take care of it when I have more energy." If someone asks you to go for a coffee, you think, "I will just make everyone depressed, I'll go when I feel better." When you no longer feel pleasure from activities you used to enjoy, you are experiencing what's known as *anhedonia*. This is a natural symptom of grief.

Anhedonia can put a real dent in your motivation to do anything. The worse you feel, the less you do. The less you do, the worse you feel. In the first few days or weeks after your loss, you may need time to process what's happened. This is not a sign of weakness. It's a sign that your heart is doing the heavy lifting of love and loss. Grief can feel like it has paused the world around you, and it's okay to move slowly as you find your footing again.

My grief is love in motion. I will be gentle with myself as my mind and body reintegrate feelings of happiness and joy.

JULY 1

CREATE A BEHAVIORAL ACTIVATION PLAN. Behavioral activation is a way of getting "unstuck" when you don't feel like doing anything. The trick is to identify super-simple activities that are pleasurable, involve social interaction, or give you a sense of accomplishment. For pleasure, you can listen to a favorite song, eat a piece of fresh fruit, or take a warm shower with your favorite shower gel. For social interaction, you can simply go pick up something from the supermarket and chat with the cashier, text a friend, or say hello to a neighbor. For accomplishment, you can choose something as simple as scheduling a doctor's appointment, cleaning your bathroom mirror, or putting away one item that's out of place. Schedule one simple activity each day this week. The goal isn't to suddenly feel great; it's to gently start somewhere—and go up from there.

Brick by brick, I build a home.

JULY 2

"Let us see to it that the recollection of those whom we have lost becomes a pleasant memory to us." —SENECA

If you opened your heart and home to a senior pet, you did something especially compassionate. Older pets are often overlooked when potential adopters are visiting a shelter. They may have come from a home where they did not receive proper care. Other times they are brought to the shelter after their human has died.

If you adopted a senior pet, you gave them a warm, loving place to land in their final chapter. That was a beautiful gift. As you grieve, it can be comforting to remember that the love you gave truly mattered.

My love for you gives me the strength to handle whatever grief decides to throw at me today.

JULY 3

MAKE YOURSELF A COMFORT MEAL TODAY. Around the world, providing food for loved ones is a way to comfort a mourner. This is because grief often robs us of time and motivation to eat a full meal. If you feel up to it, eat your favorite comfort meal tonight. If you belong to a religious congregation or community organization, consider reaching out to see if they provide this service. If a friend asks you if there's anything they can do, it's okay to suggest they drop off food or pick up some of your favorite eats from the store. A full belly can steady the heart.

I nourish myself physically, mentally, and spiritually.

JULY 4

"To live in hearts we leave behind is not to die."

—THOMAS CAMPBELL

Sometimes a pet dies very young and unexpectedly. This can happen from accidents or from sudden illness. It can be a devastating loss when you have only been together for a short time. Remember the time you did have together and how much you gave them. You took care of them, fed them, and nurtured them. You gave them the happiest and safest life you could. Cherish the joy they brought into your life, even if it was for a shorter time than you had hoped.

I cherish every single second I had with you.

JULY 5

WRITE A LETTER FROM YOUR PET TO YOU. Imagine what your pet would write to you in a letter or say to you in a phone call. Describe what you most would want to hear them say. Think about what words from them would comfort you the most. Write what they would want for you in this life. Once you've written it, read it out loud to yourself. Notice the ways you might be able to provide a generous interpretation of who you are through the eyes of your beloved animal friend.

What a gift to imagine myself through your eyes.

JULY 6

"I think I could turn and live with animals, they are so placid and self-contain[ed], I stand and look at them long and long." —WALT WHITMAN

Sometimes after the loss of a pet, we may regret not having spent more time with them. Perhaps we were busy with work, children, or taking care of an elderly relative. We wish we could do over parts of the past and devote more time to walks, give them more nutritious meals, or tell them over and over how much we love them. The beauty of our pets is that while we often get stuck in the past or future, they live fully in the present. The only expectation they had of us was to show up exactly as we were—imperfectly human, and a deep source of love. Be kind to yourself and remember all the good things that you provided for your beloved pet, day after day.

Today I will live in the present moment, without judgment.

JULY 7

NAME THE WAYS YOU SPENT QUALITY TIME WITH YOUR PET. Describe three activities that you enjoyed doing together—indoors or out. It could include observing your pet doing something, or them observing you. It could also be enjoying each other's company while doing different things, like you reading a book while they slept next to you. Bask in this pleasant memory as you imagine them nearby.

As I hold a picture of us in my mind, I feel you close by.

JULY 8

"Yet never, never can we part, while memory holds her reign."

—HENRY FRANCIS LYTE

There are other kinds of loss besides death. People may grieve after rehoming a pet due to unforeseen circumstances. We may no longer have custody of our pet due to divorce or a breakup. Whatever the reason, if you developed a bond with a pet and are now separated from them, your reaction to that loss is a form of *ambiguous grief*—grief that arises from losses that are less clear. Your grief may also be compounded if you must mourn the loss of a pet and human companion at the same time. This kind of grief can feel disorienting. Give yourself permission to feel all of it, without needing to fix or move past it too quickly. Trust that comfort will come in small, steady ways.

I release worry and stress by tolerating uncertainty.

JULY 9

WHEN GRIEF OVERWHELMS YOU, TRY THIS GROUNDING TECHNIQUE. Here, you'll use (intentional) distraction to occupy your brain so that you can break the cycle of anxious or troubling thoughts. Find a comfortable place to sit. Turn to your right and name one thing you see. Then look straight ahead and name something in front of you. Lastly, turn to your left and name something that's there. Repeat it three to four times. If you are vision-impaired, name an item that you know is in one of the three locations. This exercise should keep your mind so busy with turning and naming things that you naturally get rest from anxious thoughts. To increase the challenge, try naming the item and identifying its color.

When the world is spiraling, I root. I pause and notice safe things around me.

JULY 10

"It's the great mystery of human life that old grief passes gradually into quiet, tender joy." —FYODOR DOSTOEVSKY

As you grieve, you may notice that your reaction to your memories or external triggers will change over time. You may experience numbness. That's the brain's way of protecting you from feeling overwhelmed. You may also feel extreme sadness, anger, and an uncontrollable yearning to be with your pet. Everyone grieves on a different timeline, so managing triggers may take longer than you expected. You can start to get used to memories by spending a few minutes a day looking at photos or writing about them. As you get more comfortable reminiscing, you will feel less and less overwhelmed when the memories randomly arise.

You are now a part of me that is nurtured by my loving memories of you. You are with me wherever I go.

JULY 11

WHAT DID YOUR PET TEACH YOU? Having a pet can change us in many ways. We learn patience and how to nurture another living being. Pet companionship can help us confront uncomfortable truths about ourselves while also unleashing pride and joy. When you think about your pet, what did your relationship with them teach you? What did you learn from observing your pet's behavior? Did anything inspire a change in you?

You live on in the wisdom you gave me.

JULY 12

"Tears come from the heart, not from the brain."

—LEONARDO DA VINCI

We don't always know what's going to trigger our tears. Tears that come from strong emotions come directly from the heart. If this happens to you, and you are in a place where you feel comfortable, let your tears flow. If your tears feel "stuck," consider creating a quiet corner. No need to force tears, just set a timer for 10 to 15 minutes and allow yourself to be present with your emotions. Bring a cozy blanket, read a poem, listen to sorrowful songs—see what comes up.

Tears are a natural reaction to deeply felt loss.

JULY 13

GROUND YOURSELF WITH CALMING SCENTS. Physical sensation is a powerful way to ground into the present moment. This applies to all senses, including smell. When you're emotionally overwhelmed by thoughts of the future or past, calming or invigorating scents can bring you back to the now. Experiment with essential oils, perfume, or scented soaps and candles. You can also try natural scents such as cinnamon sticks, fresh lemon peel, flowers, pine needles, or spices. Take your time to inhale the fragrance and focus on the smell, without judgment. Notice if it makes you feel energized, relaxed, or something else entirely. You are allowed to have fun invigorating your senses.

There are many ways for me to bring myself back to the present moment.

JULY 14

"I know who I *was* when I got up this morning, but I think I must have been changed several times since then." —LEWIS CARROLL

Adjusting to life without your beloved pet can be difficult and may be marked by constantly shifting emotions. You might wake up feeling anxious, then find yourself crying uncontrollably at midday. Later, you may feel a sense of relief after the tears and find yourself sitting in quiet reflection. That evening, a friend might stop by, and you'll share a funny story about your pet—laughing together through your sadness. This emotional roller coaster can leave you feeling as bewildered as Alice in Wonderland, but it's a normal response to grief. In time, you'll begin to regulate your emotions more easily and feel a greater sense of balance.

I trust that with time steadiness will return.

JULY 15

DO SOMETHING YOU USED TO DO WITH YOUR PET. Think of any activity you have been avoiding because you either did it with your pet or they kept you company while you did it. Only do this if you feel ready. And feel free to tweak it as you reenter that physical and emotional space. For example, if you went on specific walks or hikes together, consider going there on a bike or taking a friend. If you enjoyed crosswords on the porch with your pet, take a book out there instead. When you avoid engaging in these activities that once brought you joy, you only reinforce your fears that you won't ever be able to tolerate doing them again. Gradually exposing yourself to things you used to do will help reduce anxiety.

Eventually, I will be able to engage in these activities with fond memories.

JULY 16

"Kindred spirits are not so scarce as I used to think. It's splendid to find out there are so many of them in the world." —LUCY MAUD MONTGOMERY

When you are grieving, it's important to reach out for social support. That doesn't mean always sitting and talking about your feelings or your memories. Just being in the company of other people is good enough. Even being in a place by yourself with other people around you, like a café or bookstore, can lift your mood. The key is to not isolate for long periods of time. If you are unable to leave your home, reach out to people via your typical forms of communication. Sometimes comfort really is only a phone call away.

Humans are social animals. When I embrace human connection, I open my heart.

JULY 17

MAKE TIME TO BE AROUND HUMANS TODAY. Going to the movies is a great option, even if you go alone. You will be surrounded by other people, which is what's important. If you'd rather be around those you know, invite a friend, family member, or neighbor to spend time with you today. Consider somewhere neutral, like a coffee shop, where you are free to leave at any time. Give yourself permission to take a break from grieving.

I deserve moments of connection and lightness.

JULY 18

"Memory is the treasury and guardian of all things." –CICERO

Our pets often touch the lives of other people in our life. Our family, friends, and neighbors likely got to know certain aspects of them. It can be comforting to hear their memories of our pet—to see our animal companion through their eyes. It's also a way of acknowledging the role they played beyond your own home, in the broader community they were a part of.

Collective memory allows for collective healing. When I am ready, I will remember with others.

JULY 19

ASK FOR ANECDOTES FROM OTHER PEOPLE WHO KNEW YOUR PET. If you are ready, reach out to other people who knew your pet, such as family members, friends, or neighbors. Ask them what impression they had of your pet. See if they have any stories to share. Consider adding these to a memory book, so you can read them in the future. If this feels overwhelming, or unsafe with certain people, give yourself permission to postpone or forgo these interactions.

With each new story, I learn more about you.

JULY 20

"[She's] so spicy, I named her Pepper."

—KACEY MUSGRAVES, ABOUT HER DOG, PEPPER

Our pet's names have a lot of significance to us. We may spend hours and days trying to come up with just the right name. Other times, the minute we meet our pet for the first time, we know exactly what to call them. Not all animals recognize their name, but if your pet was one who did, there may have been great pleasure when they responded to it.

A name forever holds love, memory, and meaning. Speaking it keeps them close to the bone.

JULY 21

HOW DID YOU CHOOSE YOUR PET'S NAME? Think about the process that you went through to come up with your pet's name. Is there a funny story associated with it? Describe the ways your pet responded to their name. Did your pet have their name on any items, such as a water dish, brush, or blanket? Did they have any special nicknames?

Your name tells a story only we shared.

JULY 22

"Grief has a strange power in opening the hearts of those who sorrow in common." —DONALD G. MITCHELL

Caring for a sick pet or grieving the loss of a pet can have an impact on relationships. Family members or partners may be at odds about treatment decisions, leaving either or both feeling unseen. There can also be conflict and blame if the pet was injured in an accident, ran away, or was stolen. Because the experience of grief is unique for each grieving person, there may be disagreement about how your pet's memory should be honored. Speaking openly and honestly with each other is key. This is an opportunity to grow closer and support each other.

Even if we grieve differently, our love for our pet was shared. I can honor my truth while holding space for theirs.

JULY 23

PRACTICE ACTIVE LISTENING. Active listening is a valuable technique that makes conversation more meaningful and productive. If there's someone you've had conflict with regarding the care and loss of your pet, ask them to sit with you for a few minutes. Let them speak without interrupting. Really focus on what they're saying. Resist thinking ahead to what you'll say next. Simply listen.

Once they're done, echo back what they said so they feel truly heard. Now express how you feel. Allow each person to offer a resolution, again without interrupting or mentally preparing a response while the other speaks. The resolution may simply be a greater understanding of each other's love for your animal. This is a simple overview, but the key is to take turns while remaining open and nonjudgmental. If you feel your heart rate rise during this exercise, take a loving pause.

In this tender time, compassion matters more than agreement.

JULY 24

"[T]he very joys of others make my sorrows more intolerable!" —THOMAS H. CHIVERS, IN A LETTER TO EDGAR ALLAN POE

In the beginning, it may be hard to be around other animals. I had a client, Jim, who couldn't tolerate being around dogs after he lost his beloved JoJo. It didn't matter if it was a dog he knew, or one he passed on the street. "I don't want to have anything to do with them," he said. "None of them are my JoJo." Jim said he still loved dogs, of course, but when he saw other people having fun with theirs, it was just a reminder of how unfair it felt. I explained this was a very normal reaction to losing a pet. Jim needed more time to process his loss. He gradually began to engage in activities and socialize with friends. Several weeks later he came back in with a slightly different tune: "I got some pets in with my friend's dog today. It's not the same as petting JoJo, but it still felt nice."

Like Jim, it may take time for you to be around other animals. Give yourself permission to feel that resistance. Your heart is protecting itself, and in its own time, it may begin to open again—softly, and when you're ready.

All emotions are valid and part of being human. I can choose what I do with those emotions, and that's what counts.

JULY 25

INCREASE YOUR COMFORT LEVEL AROUND ANIMALS. When you are ready, consider some of these gradual exposure techniques. You might begin by simply observing animals at a park or on a walking trail—no need to interact, just notice. When you're comfortable, you can try short visits with friends or family who have pets. These can be brief and on your terms. You don't even have to engage with the animal, just being nearby is enough. Over time, you can gradually increase the length and frequency of visits and begin to interact with the animals when you feel ready.

It's important to go at your own pace. There's no need to rush or push yourself. If it still feels too hard after a few tries, it's okay to pause and come back to it later. Compassion for yourself is the most important step.

I listen closely to my heart and move at a pace that's comfortable for me.

JULY 26

"An animal's eyes have the power to speak a great language." —MARTIN BUBER

Some animals offer more than companionship. They become our emotional anchors, our daily support, our quiet co-regulators. Whether your pet was a trained therapy or service animal, or simply offered you a deep sense of comfort, safety, or purpose, their loss can leave a profound emptiness. You may be grieving not only a beloved companion but also a source of grounding, structure, or meaning in your life. Your loss is valid, layered, and worthy of time and care.

Your presence shaped my life in ways I will always carry.

JULY 27

HOW DID YOUR PET PROVIDE EMOTIONAL SUPPORT TO YOU OR OTHERS? Describe ways that your pet provided emotional support to you. Consider how they helped you de-stress, quiet anger, or ease sadness. Think about other people your pet spent time with. How did your pet provide emotional support to them? If you had a therapy pet, jot down some of your shared experiences.

I am learning new ways to support myself emotionally, starting with sweet memories of you.

JULY 28

“He who has felt the deepest grief is best able to experience supreme happiness.” —ALEXANDRE DUMAS

When you are grieving the loss of a beloved pet, it does not mean that you are only allowed to feel sad, painful emotions. You are not disrespecting the memory of your pet by feeling happy or thinking about the future. It is possible to yearn for them, while also allowing pockets of happiness into your life.

I allow joy and sorrow to coexist in my heart.

JULY 29

NAME THREE THINGS ON YOUR LONG-TERM GOAL LIST. When you are ready, write down three dreams or experiences you've always said you'd pursue "someday"—whether that's traveling somewhere new, learning a creative skill, or making a meaningful change in your life. Grief often narrows our world; imagining the future can gently reopen it. You might even create a small vision board, collage, or notes jar to represent these hopes—not as a source of pressure to move on, but as a quiet reminder that possibility still exists. Let this be an invitation to begin looking forward, even if just a little.

I am allowed to dream, even while I grieve.

JULY 30

"In the hour of adversity be not without hope, for crystal rain falls from black clouds." —NIZAMI GANJAVI

It may be hard to imagine feeling anything but the deep pain you are in right now. There is no way to predict how long the intensity of your pain will last. But the fact that you are reading these words means you've begun to look for healthy ways to manage your grief. It means you have hope.

Hope is a buoy in this dark ocean.

JULY 31

TRY AFFIRMATIONS TO HELP COPE WITH YOUR LOSS. Saying something affirming or comforting out loud can help you cope with grief. Try repeating affirmations to yourself when you wake up, or if you are feeling overwhelmed by emotions during the day. You can create your own affirmations or search for ones that speak to you. (There are many for you to choose from in this book, including a few extra today!) Use affirmations that resonate with you—avoid anything that doesn't feel true. Here are a few to have on hand:

I am kind to myself as I navigate the grieving process.

It is okay if I take a break from grieving.

I am resilient and can manage the pain.

I hold my beloved pet in my heart.

AUGUST 1

". . . The best way out is always through." —ROBERT FROST

Learning different models of grief can help make sense of the profound nature of pet loss. One model that's especially helpful for pet loss is J. William Worden's "Four Tasks of Mourning." The tasks include:

1. Accepting the reality of the loss.
2. Processing the pain of grief.
3. Adjusting to a world without the deceased.
4. Finding an enduring connection with the deceased while embarking on a new life.

You can engage in these tasks separately or simultaneously, and they can be revisited or reworked over time.

When I learn more about the grieving process, I support the different layers of my experience.

AUGUST 2

REFLECT ON WHERE YOU ARE IN THE ACCEPTANCE PORTION OF YOUR GRIEVING JOURNEY. An important task of mourning is to accept the reality of your loss. The timeline for this is different for each person. Acceptance does not mean that you have resolved your loss emotionally, it just means that you are able to digest the fact that it happened. Activities that support acceptance include talking about the significance of the loss, attending rituals that acknowledge the loss, and creating a memorial or altar in the home.

Acceptance is not easy, but it is part of my healing journey.

AUGUST 3

"The greatest happiness of life is the conviction that we are loved—loved for ourselves, or rather, loved in spite of ourselves." —VICTOR HUGO

Pets have many ways of showing affection for their humans. Maybe yours followed you around or kept an eye on you from a distance. They might have loved your scent and curled up with anything that smelled just like you. Maybe they vocalized their love as soon as they saw you. When you're missing your pet, this love and affection may be what you miss the most. Take a moment to embrace the memories of feeling loved by your pet. Welcome it fully like a warm embrace.

Thank you for loving me for all that I am.

AUGUST 4

TRY TO PINPOINT YOUR PET'S FAVORITE ITEM OF YOURS. Many animals love the smell of their caregivers. Did you find yours curling up near your hamper? Were they fond of sniffing your shoes or dirty socks? Did they steal a beloved possession when you weren't looking? Describe any item they loved, especially in times when they needed comfort. To feel closer to them, place this item near you or where you can see it.

They found comfort in my scent, just as I now find comfort in their memory. Our connection lives on in small, familiar things.

AUGUST 5

"The advice I give to all adventurers is to seek a place where they may sleep in safety." —SAMUEL DE CHAMPLAIN

Many of the animals that we care for are prey animals. Providing a sense of safety for them is critical for their well-being. One of the sweetest ways our pets can show they trust us is by sleeping near us or on us, depending on the species. It's in those restful, vulnerable moments when you perhaps felt the most tenderness toward them—watching them twitch as they ran in their dreams or dangle comically from their favorite perch. It works both ways.

We also felt loved and safe when our pets were snuggled up with us. It may be hard at first to fall asleep without your pet. Some people find comfort in saying "good night" to their pet's photo or ashes or sleeping with something that belonged to them. Do whatever you need to do to feel close to them as you tuck yourself in tonight.

The quiet moments we shared still live in my heart.

AUGUST 6

WHERE DID YOUR PET LIKE TO SLEEP? Describe where your pet slept at night or during the day. Write about the positions that they slept in and make sure to include all the funny ones. If you had a horse, they probably slept standing up most of the time, but did you ever catch them taking a short nap on the ground? If you had a bird, did you cover their cage when it was time to sleep? If your pet slept with you, describe how they woke up in the morning.

As I rest, I carry your warmth with me.

AUGUST 7

"Few delights can equal the mere presence of one whom we trust utterly." —GEORGE MACDONALD

Only when our animals trust us fully, will they let us hold them. This connection releases oxytocin, the bond-building hormone released during acts of physical tenderness, intimacy, and between mothers and newborns. This may come as no surprise as pets often feel like our babies. Depending on the size of your pet, they may have loved to sit in your lap or be cradled in your arms. If your pet was small, maybe they climbed or crawled on you. If your pet was large, just putting your arms around their neck for a nuzzle felt connective. Missing this physical closeness can be one of the most painful aspects of parting with our beloved.

Thank you for every loving touch.

AUGUST 8

FIND SOMETHING TO HUG. Comfort from a pet comes in many forms. It is normal to long for that physical connection once it's gone. Try cuddling a stuffed animal when the pain feels acute. You can also use a throw pillow, the squishier the better. Some people like to hug a toy or a blanket that belonged to their pet. Just the feeling of hugging something can bring a sense of calm and comfort, helping to regulate distressing emotions.

Each hug is a step toward healing and a reminder that love still surrounds me.

AUGUST 9

"Grief, and the possibility of it, are what make life precious. Grief, therefore, has profound value." —H. A. OVERSTREET

The great irony of the human-animal bond is that we open our hearts knowing we will eventually grieve their departure. We do so because we know this love is worth the pain. And still, this loss can blindside us. Animals bring meaning and purpose into our lives—after all, they depend on us for safety, food, shelter, and love. After losing a pet, it can feel like life has lost some sense of meaning. By examining what matters most to you, you will gradually start to engage in things that bring meaning to your life again.

Honoring what I value will guide me to my purpose.

AUGUST 10

IDENTIFY WHAT MATTERS MOST TO YOU. When you are ready to start engaging in new activities, take 30 minutes to sit down and think about what you value most. You can break this up into categories like health, family, work, community, relationships, and personal growth. Identify the two most important areas to you. Pick one thing you can do in each area that you have not done in a while. For example, if family is important to you, call your sister. If health is an important value, eat a nutritious meal. Doing activities that align with your values can bring a sense of relief, enjoyment, and satisfaction.

I take time to gently reconnect to what matters most to me.

AUGUST 11

"Grief was my master yesternight;
To-morrow I may grieve again; But now along the windy plain, The clouds have taken flight." —ARCHIBALD LAMPMAN

There may be days when your grief is overwhelming. You may have trouble sleeping or feel unable to get out of bed. Then there may be a day you wake up and feel like the heavy weight of grief has lifted, if only slightly. The intensity and frequency of this fluctuation can be frustrating. Grief is an opportunity to learn skills that can help you cope with strong emotions. The most important thing to know is that all emotions are valid and a natural part of grief.

I can manage my grief, even if it's overwhelming. I know that it will not always be as intense as its worst day.

AUGUST 12

EXPRESS YOUR ANGER IN A HEALTHY WAY. Anger often accompanies grief. Letting it out can help you release the parts of that energy that don't serve you—and work as a safeguard against erupting in hurtful ways later. Reducing stress also helps shift your nervous system out of fight-or-flight mode. Here are a few ways to safely release your anger:

EXERCISE. Try kickboxing, playing an intense game, or running.

WRITE IT OUT. Jot down what you're angry about. Maybe it's your spouse, the driver in front of you, or even the color of the grass today. There's no wrong explanation. Don't hold back.

SOOTHE YOURSELF. Try meditation, yoga, or breathing exercises.

Anger is a natural part of the grieving process. I find ways to release it safely.

AUGUST 13

"We all experience loss at some point in our lives . . . Being able to really SIT in this grief allows you to feel the moments of joy and gratitude for having loved someone that deep." —JENNIFER ANISTON

One question I hear fairly frequently from my clients is, "What if I can't remember my pet?" This is a reasonable question, especially shortly after the loss, when you may be focused only on traumatic memories of their final days. If you are experiencing grief over this loss, that indicates that you had a strong bond with your pet and are not likely to forget them. What can also help is to engage in activities like writing or talking about your memories. We live in a time where it's easy to record photos and videos of our pets. Even if we forget a detail, we have plenty of references to look back on and enjoy.

I have many ways to remember and stay connected to my beloved pet.

AUGUST 14

TELL YOUR PET HOW MUCH YOU MISS THEM. Sit in a quiet, comfortable place and close your eyes. Imagine that your pet is in front of you. Describe the activities you miss doing with them. Thank them for being such an important part of your life. Tell them what you plan to do to honor their memory and keep them close to your heart. After you've finished, take a few deep breaths. If you'd like to hold on to this moment, journal about the experience.

My imagination is a powerful tool to keep memories alive and strengthen our bond.

AUGUST 15

"To weep is to make less the depths of grief."

—WILLIAM SHAKESPEARE

The pain of losing a pet can be so overpowering that you may want to avoid it completely. The catch-22? Avoidance prolongs grief. By leaning into your grief, you can begin to acknowledge that the loss has happened and that there are aspects of your life that have changed. This will likely bring up some sharp feelings, so it's okay if you want to do this gradually. You will develop skills to manage those feelings over time. Several of these skills like journaling, grounding exercises, and stress reduction are in this book. As you move through grief, you will start to ease back into life. In other words, you will build resilience.

I can choose to expose myself to the pain of grief in gradual, manageable doses.

AUGUST 16

PRACTICE EMOTIONAL OBJECTIVITY. One way to ease the discomfort of processing your emotions is to take a step back and look at them objectively. Pretend you are writing an online review about Grief, Inc.—as if your grief were a place you were visiting. Name each emotion you experienced there and how those emotions made you react. Write what you did or didn't like about those feelings. Then rate Grief, Inc., on a 10-point scale, with 1 being "awful" and 10 being "the best." Example: "I went to Grief, Inc., and was angry and sad. I couldn't stop crying and my chest hurt. I hated it. I did feel a little better after a good cry, though. I give it a 4 out of 10."

Creativity is a powerful ally in healing. By giving my emotions shape and a story, I create space to understand and soften them.

AUGUST 17

"The spirit of self-help is the root of all genuine growth in the individual." —SAMUEL SMILES

Many people who grieve find that they experience personal growth as time passes. For example, as they adjust to life following the loss of their beloved pet, they may discover what matters most to them. They may have a greater appreciation for the preciousness of life and spend more time with loved ones, including other pets. They may also develop a sense of purpose as they find ways to honor their pet, such as getting involved with a rescue organization or developing a new creative or athletic hobby.

I find ways to embrace joy, adventure, and growth in your honor.

AUGUST 18

MAKE AN ACTIVITY SCHEDULE FOR THIS WEEK. When you are grieving, you might have days that you feel stuck. Scheduling activities in advance can give you something to look forward to. (You'll be more likely to do them if they're already on the calendar.) This week, pick two activities that are pleasant or productive. They shouldn't require too much effort or take up more than an hour. Schedule them at a fixed day and time. For extra motivation, ask a friend or relative to join you. If the time comes and you don't feel up to it, try to push yourself a little while honoring your needs and boundaries.

Even simple activities are quiet acts of hope.

AUGUST 19

"My Pearly girl will be with me forever in the softest place in my heart, where I cherish all the people who have left but whom I still feel every day."

—JENNIE GARTH, ABOUT HER LATE DOG, PEARL

There is much you can do to tend to the soft space of your heart, preparing it like you would a bed to rest your head. You can do this through commemoration rituals, meaningful activities, or sharing stories that bring warmth. It's possible to find an enduring connection with your pet while embarking on a new version of your life. That tender place has an infinite capacity for affection. And there's plenty of room for every being you've ever loved and lost to reside there.

There is infinite space for you in my heart, not dependent on time or love for anyone else.

AUGUST 20

CREATE MEMORIAL STONES FOR YOUR PET. Memorial stones are small rocks where you paint your pet's name and, if you like, a message. Consider carrying a memorial stone with you when you are grieving. You can also display them in your home, office, or any place you used to share with your animal. If your pet went outdoors, you can distribute them in places where they liked to play or explore.

Acts of remembrance honor the bond that was shared and mindfully carries the spirit forward.

AUGUST 21

"I'm really a very happy, contented little person in spite of my broken heart." —LUCY MAUD MONTGOMERY

Resilience is the ability to adapt to adversity. We build resilience starting in childhood and can continue strengthening it throughout our lifetime. In her podcast *The Resilience Reset*, psychiatrist Dr. Tracey Marks explains that you can do this by "strengthening your mind and fortifying your brain." As you experience grief and adjust to your loss, you can strengthen your mind by talking or writing about how you're feeling, learning mindfulness techniques, and engaging in positive self-talk. You can further strengthen your body's capacity to deal with stress by getting good sleep, mindfully eating, and exercising.

My resilience is a reminder of my capacity to heal and grow.

AUGUST 22

WHAT WAS YOUR GREATEST CHALLENGE IN LIFE? Think about the challenge that you are most proud of overcoming. Describe what it took to see yourself through this challenge. List any people who supported you and what you told yourself during this time. Identifying what got you through that difficult period can serve as a useful reminder of your strength in this moment. You've pulled through before, and you will pull through again.

I trust in my capacity to build resilience, little by little, day by day.

AUGUST 23

"And as spirit is the foundation of courage, such natures, whether of [hu]mans or animals, will be full of spirit."

—PLATO

Honoring your pet's courage can help you manage your grief. Many rescue animals have faced hardship before their adoption into safe homes; they may have survived a natural disaster or overcome abuse. Dogs who are frontline or therapeutic workers do everything from sniffing landmines to aiding rehabilitation. Despite what your animal saw or endured, their love for you demonstrated their deep capacity for trust and love. Sharing stories of your pet's bravery can help keep their memory alive, strengthen your bond with them, and inspire others.

Our love was an act of courage, because there was always the promise of loss.

AUGUST 24

CONSIDER HELPING A RETIRED OR RESCUED ANIMAL. One way to honor your pet's memory is to support animals in need of care later in life. This can include retired working animals—like service dogs, military or police K9s, therapy animals, or farm animals—who deserve a peaceful retirement. There are also sanctuaries and rescue organizations that care for older or special-needs animals. Donating, volunteering, or simply spreading the word can be a meaningful tribute to your pet.

I find meaningful ways to honor your memory.

AUGUST 25

"Laughter and tears are meant to turn the wheels of the same machinery of sensibility; one is wind power and the other water power, that is all." —OLIVER WENDELL HOLMES SR.

It's okay to laugh when you're grieving. You don't have to be solemn every moment. Just like tears, laughter helps us release emotion. It also relieves stress and uplifts one's mood. Laughing doesn't erase your feelings of pain; it reflects the natural complexity of your emotions. Every day of grieving will look and feel different. It's okay to take a break from your sorrow.

I honor your memory with both tears and laughter.

AUGUST 26

MAKE TIME FOR THERAPEUTIC LAUGHTER. This week, try giving yourself a laugh break. Watch your favorite comic's stand-up special. Stream a funny podcast or binge your favorite lighthearted show. Reach out to a trusted friend and ask them to send you their favorite memes. There is no wrong way to laugh. Find whatever tickles your soul and lean into it.

If nothing feels funny, evidence suggests that even forced, fake laughter has positive mood-regulation benefits. In the practice of laughing yoga, participants engage in prolonged, simulated laughter to promote relaxation and release stress. To try your hand at laughing yoga, start by taking slow, deep breaths. Release laughter intentionally, pulling it up from your diaphragm, focusing on the action rather than waiting for a reason to laugh. In most cases, genuine laughter soon follows.

Laughter is a natural way to soothe myself.

AUGUST 27

"[One who] lacks time to mourn, lacks time to mend."

—SIR HENRY TAYLOR

Giving yourself time to mourn doesn't mean stopping everything else for days or weeks. With a little practice, it is possible to dedicate some time for yourself, even if it's just a few minutes here and there. In these small moments, you can reflect on your loss, maybe writing in a journal or talking to a friend. Giving yourself time, even in micro-doses, will help mend your heart.

In small moments, I create space for my grief. In those spaces, I begin to mend.

AUGUST 28

SET A REGULAR TIME TO MOURN. Dedicating time to engage with your emotions begins to create feelings of safety around this process. In other words, the more you show up for yourself, the easier it gets—and the more you get out of it with less input. You can use this time to write, talk to someone, reminisce, or, of course, cry. It's not how much time you choose to set aside; that will vary. It's about the consistency of allowing room for yourself to open, reflect, and release.

I find safety and security in the gentle consistency of ritual.

AUGUST 29

"Towards the end I found myself calling him "Puppy" as if to recall happier times and maybe stave off the inevitable . . . It is never easy."

—CHRISTOPHER MELONI, ABOUT HIS LATE DOG, SCOTTY

Research from scientists in Japan who study the power of *kawaii,* or "cuteness" in Japanese, suggest that viewing images of baby animals boosts focus, fine motor skills, and even athletic performance. It's true: Nothing says joy quite like a group of baby animals frolicking together. Young animals can be a handful to raise, but it's usually worth the effort (and mayhem!).

If you welcomed your pet into your life when they were a baby, try to remember what that season was like. What did they look like? What funny or chaotic things did they do? If your pet came to you later in life, try imagining what they might have been like as a baby. Reflecting on those early moments can bring a bittersweet kind of joy, the kind that honors the full arc of your pet's life and your love.

I treasure the full arc of your life.

AUGUST 30

WHAT SORT OF MISCHIEF DID YOUR PET GET INTO? Describe a time when your pet's curiosity got the best of them. Maybe they were in a part of your home that was off-limits. Or they managed to get at their food or treats in between meals. Perhaps, a few pairs of socks or other items went missing. If your pet was always on their best behavior, spend a few moments today thinking about the other ways they made you laugh or brought joy into your life.

There is joy in a little bit of mischief. Thank you for your playful shenanigans!

AUGUST 31

"Like a plant that starts up in showers and sunshine and does not know which has best helped it to grow, it is difficult to say whether the hard things or the pleasant things did me the most good." —LUCY LARCOM

Although grief is inherently painful, it is also inevitably interlaced with the beauty of life. As grief begins to lift, we might see how we've grown or learned from our loss. This should not be confused with toxic positivity, which invalidates negative emotions or difficult experiences. Grieving, while categorically unpleasant, tends to unlock a greater appreciation for life and can draw people closer to their values. They might strengthen relationships with people or spirituality or end those relationships that no longer serve them. How you grieve is up to you, as is how you praise the life before you.

Healing does not mean denying the pain.

SEPTEMBER 1

WHAT'S THE MOST IMPORTANT THING YOU'VE LEARNED FROM YOUR GRIEF SO FAR? Take a moment to think about what you have learned since you started grieving your pet. Examine what your emotional and physical reaction has been. Have you found any helpful coping skills? Consider insights you've gained about life or death. Describe what you have learned from interactions with other people. Grief is a time of transformation; acknowledging this can offer you a long-term perspective. If you feel it's too soon for this activity, you can return to it at a later date.

Grief is reshaping me. With each insight, I grow stronger and more compassionate.

SEPTEMBER 2

“The very ocean of tears has its other shore, else none would have ever wept.” —RABINDRANATH TAGORE

Water is essential for our existence. Our vital organs, including the heart, are made mostly of water. If you think about it, it’s amazing that our own body uses water as a form of emotional expression. Tears express sadness or joy. Cultures all over the world honor water as a source of life and healing. Your tears serve an important purpose by allowing you to express deep emotion. Trust them.

I can let my tears flow without drowning.

SEPTEMBER 3

CONNECT WITH THE CALMING POWER OF WATER. Listen to ambient sounds of rain or ocean waves. Watch documentaries or travel videos about waterfalls and oceans. If you live near water, consider visiting the shore or even taking a boat ride. If there isn’t natural water nearby, a bubble bath or leisurely shower can bring the sensations of calmness or oneness.

I am made of water and water is mutable.

SEPTEMBER 4

"I usually find myself among strangers because I drift here and there trying to forget the sad thing that happened to me."

—F. SCOTT FITZGERALD

Spending time with loved ones and friends can provide support while you're grieving. Sometimes, though, you may want to take a break from grieving and be around people who don't know you. They won't ask you questions that you're not ready to answer. They don't even know that you ever had a pet. There is power in anonymity. You get to decide whether and how to interact with strangers for whom you're but another face in the crowd.

I embrace the peace of solitude. I can take a break from grieving whenever I need to.

SEPTEMBER 5

VISIT A NEARBY TOWN WHERE NOBODY KNOWS YOU. Take the day to be anonymous. Explore new stores, parks, or cafés. Go where you are unlikely to run into anyone you know. You can also choose to take a day trip somewhere new. Spend time just enjoying your surroundings. If you are feeling sociable, consider striking up a conversation with someone you meet. You can also sign up for a class or take a walking tour where you can interact with new people.

I choose when, where, and how to grieve.

SEPTEMBER 6

"Animals not only love, but have the desire to be loved."

—CHARLES DARWIN

The bond that you and your pet created together was built on love. You showed how much you loved them by providing attention, play, food, and shelter, helping them feel safe and protected. They returned the love in the form of loyalty and affection, which you received with joy. That reciprocity is what made your connection so meaningful. Unlike with some humans, you didn't have reason to doubt whether your pet's affection was genuine. That sense of deeply unconditional love is something you can continue to cultivate within yourself.

You showed me that I can love and be loved.

SEPTEMBER 7

WHAT WERE SOME OF YOUR PET'S VERY FAVORITE TREATS? Make a list of the foods your pet loved to eat. Include any treats they enjoyed on special occasions. Describe the human foods they might try to steal off your plate. If your pet was a picky eater, make sure to write about that, too.

It was my job, and my delight, to nourish you.

SEPTEMBER 8

"Life is a shadowy, strange, and winding road."

—ROBERT G. INGERSOLL

You may have had plans for the future with your beloved pet—places you hoped to go or experiences you looked forward to sharing. Perhaps there were life milestones you imagined celebrating with them by your side. Grieving the loss of these hopes or feeling regret for what you didn't get to do together is a normal response to loss. It may help to find symbolic ways to include your pet in future activities and milestones, keeping their memory present as your life continues to unfold.

You are a part of me now. Wherever I go, you go with me.

SEPTEMBER 9

MAKE A PLAN TO INCLUDE YOUR PET IN IMPORTANT FUTURE EVENTS. You may have events coming up this year that you had hoped your pet could be part of. Pick a significant one and think of how you might still be able to involve them. You can wear a keepsake like a locket on the special day or bring along an item that belonged to them if you're traveling. If you're hosting a celebration at home, find a creative way to include them, such as putting their photos in party decorations or even at the table so they can join you for the meal.

Your presence lives on in the moments that matter.

SEPTEMBER 10

"However long the night, the dawn will break."

—AFRICAN PROVERB

Grief keeps its own rhythm. The pain can make it feel like you're trapped in a dark, endless night. In moments of despair, hold on to the truth that there is no such thing as an endless night. There is always daybreak. As you allow the grieving process to take its natural course, there will be days ahead with a little less pain and sadness, and even some moments of joy. You may always miss your pet, but you will find ways of carrying their light with you as you move through and out of the darkness.

I am moving through this grief, not standing still in it.

SEPTEMBER 11

BLOW SOAP BUBBLES TO GROUND YOURSELF. No matter your age, this fun activity grounds you by slowing down your breath and mindfully concentrating on the present moment. If possible, go outside and watch your bubbles float in the breeze. Spending just a few minutes blowing bubbles can relax your nervous system. If this is an activity you enjoyed with your pet, it may bring back pleasant memories. If the reminder is too painful for now, you can come back to this activity when you are ready.

With each breath, I find calm, lightness, a place to just be.

SEPTEMBER 12

"Sweet, cheerful words, coming from a kind heart, are worth more than gold and gems." —ROSELLA RICE

In the quiet corners of grief, there's a solace in kind words. They can come from someone you know, a stranger, or even yourself. Perhaps the words are in a card, a poem, or a song lyric. Very often, it's the simplest statements that provide the most comfort—someone writing to say, "I am thinking of you." Surrounding yourself with kind words, including the ones in your own head, will help you feel safe and able to cope with strong tides of emotion.

I welcome kind words into my life.

SEPTEMBER 13

USE POSITIVE SELF-TALK THROUGHOUT THE DAY. Have you ever sent an email without an attachment, or gone to the store to pick up something only to come back with everything but that item? If so, you may have said something like, "I'm such a dummy, what's wrong with me?" That kind of speech is negative self-talk, and it can bring down our mood and reduce self-confidence.

Throughout the day today, talk to yourself like you are your own best friend. Give yourself a verbal "Great job!" when you complete a task. If you make a mistake, say, "Oh well, mistakes happen." Take a look in the mirror and greet yourself by saying, "Good morning, it's nice to see you today." See how you feel by the end of the day; if you like the results, try it for a week.

Today, I prioritize self-kindness.

SEPTEMBER 14

"That is one good thing about this world . . . there are always sure to be more springs." —LUCY MAUD MONTGOMERY

Helplessness is one of the emotions that can appear when you are grieving, especially in the initial weeks after your loss. Sometimes this helplessness is accompanied by anger and frustration. These are natural responses to grief. Perhaps you've thought you should've been able to do something to save your pet, which can activate feelings of helplessness and shame. You can challenge these beliefs by noting your strengths, starting with the enduring empathy you had for your pet.

My care, compassion, and effort were acts of deep love.

SEPTEMBER 15

MAKE A LIST OF YOUR STRENGTHS. Take an inventory of your strengths to bolster beliefs about your worthiness and competence. Start with the abilities that allowed you to care for your pet—consider kindness, responsibility, empathy, loyalty, and attentiveness. Add any other strengths that come to mind. Poll family and friends to round out your list. Jot down each strength you land on and refer to them for the next three days. Take note of how you feel at the end of these three days. Has anything shifted?

My strengths are real and lasting. I am capable and growing, even in grief.

SEPTEMBER 16

“Those who grieve, find comfort in weeping and in arousing their sorrow until the body is too tired to bear the inner emotions.” —MAIMONIDES

Feeling tired and stressed is common during the grieving process. This is especially true if you've been caring for a terminally ill pet. You may also have trouble sleeping—whether from the shock of the loss or the unfamiliarity of sleeping without your pet by your side. At other times, exhaustion may come from the emotional toll of managing intense feelings. It can be helpful to take a break from grieving and do something calming that requires very little effort on your part, such as getting a massage.

I embrace relaxation and rest as healing mechanisms.

SEPTEMBER 17

TAKE IT EASY TODAY. Carve out “me time” during the day today. It can be for three minutes or the entire day. Put your feet up and read a book or binge-watch a show you like. Make a bowl of ice cream and savor each bite. If you have a busy home or not much privacy, walk to a quiet place, such as a library or a park bench to just be.

It's okay to give myself a break when I'm emotionally taxed.

SEPTEMBER 18

"A thing of beauty is a joy forever." —JOHN KEATS

There may have been times that you sat and observed your pet playing, sleeping, or engaging with the world and simply marveled at them. Research from the Human Animal Bond Research Institute indicates that human-animal interaction can increase oxytocin levels in the brain, creating a sense of calm, comfort, and focus. In other words, these moments brought a sense of peace, and you're likely missing them now. As you process your grief, you may eventually feel a calming effect simply by remembering these pleasant times with your animal companion.

The peace I felt with my pet still lives in my memories.

SEPTEMBER 19

WHAT MADE YOUR PET BEAUTIFUL? Describe what you found most beautiful about your pet. Was it their fuzzy ears? The elegant way they moved? Did they jump without making a sound? Think about these details and note if you feel their presence.

As I remember you, I allow comfort to return, gently and steadily.

SEPTEMBER 20

"Joy is the ray of sunshine that brightens and opens those two beautiful flowers, Confidence and Hope."

—É. SOUVESTRE

My sweet tuxedo cat Joni was the embodiment of joy. She'd run to the door to greet any visitors who might drop in, even the super. One time, I picked her up from boarding and noticed she looked a little heavier. The receptionist told me, "Everybody here has been sneaking her treats, she's so sweet!"

When I was grieving, I would think of the joy Joni brought to others and worked to emulate that friendliness in my own interactions. Remembering her best qualities in difficult moments gave me a sense of emotional confidence because I knew I was summoning the purest parts of her being to come alive in me. In remembering the positive values our pets taught us, we can reflect those attributes in our daily life and, in so doing, extend our bond.

The joy my pet brought to the world lives on through me.

SEPTEMBER 21

BE INSPIRED BY YOUR PET'S BEST QUALITIES. Think about what you admired about your pet and let that inspire you this week. For example, if they demonstrated courage, tackle something difficult this week. If they were very curious, spend some time learning something new and unexpected. If they were athletic, try a new exercise class or go for a walk. Keep them in mind as you do these activities. In this way, you both honor their memory and incorporate them into your daily life as it goes on.

You inspire me to be my best self.

SEPTEMBER 22

"There is nothing stronger than these two: Patience and Time." —LEO TOLSTOY

Your life has changed because of your loss, and you may need time to find your bearings. For that reason, it's usually a good idea to postpone making any major life decisions. Have patience until you feel you are in the right mindset for decision-making. In the meantime, focus on engaging in activities that help you process your grief.

There is a time to act, and a time to reflect.

SEPTEMBER 23

CREATE A SMALL KEEPSAKE TO CARRY WITH YOU. Carrying a reminder of your pet with you can be a deeply comforting act. You might tuck a small photo into your wallet, draw a tiny portrait on a piece of card stock, or write their name and a short message on a slip of paper. Keep it in your pocket, bag, locket, key chain, or beside your bed—anywhere it brings you a sense of closeness. In this way, your pet stays near, a quiet presence in your daily life.

I carry your love with me wherever I go.

SEPTEMBER 24

"Not as my sorrow, but as the sorrow of the world; not a personal isolating pain, but a pain without bitterness that unites all humanity." —C. G. JUNG

There are millions of people around the world who are grieving at this moment. They are grieving every kind of loss, including the loss of a beloved animal companion. That doesn't mean that everyone processes their grief in the same way—that's impossible because grief is unique to each love it reflects. But it's important to remember that loss is a part of the human condition, and that you are connected to a network of people on a similar journey. Imagine yourself in good company.

Grief is a part of the human experience. I am not alone.

SEPTEMBER 25

TRY A LOVING-KINDNESS MEDITATION. Loving-kindness meditation is based on the Buddhist concept of metta, which extends compassion to yourself, others you know, and all of humanity.

1. Take 10 minutes and sit quietly and comfortably. Close your eyes if you feel safe doing so.
2. Take a few slow breaths and relax your body.
3. Say out loud or in your mind the following statements, slowly and intentionally: “May I be happy, may I be safe, may I be healthy, may I be at peace.” Take another slow inhale and exhale. Repeat this three times.
4. Then, think of a loved one and say, “May you be happy, may you be safe, may you be healthy, may you be at peace.”
5. Next, think of people you don’t know that well or don’t like and repeat the same statement three times.
6. For the last round, think of all creatures around the world and say, “May all creatures be happy, may all creatures be safe, may all creatures be healthy, may all creatures be at peace.” Take a few more deep breaths, wiggle your fingers or toes, and open your eyes. Try this once a week for the next three weeks.

I am a being of compassion.

SEPTEMBER 26

"I am not afraid of storms, for I am learning to sail my ship."

—LOUISA MAY ALCOTT

It's important to pace yourself while you are grieving. Though the pain may feel unsurmountable at times, remember that like a tidal wave, it naturally subsides when we let it follow its course. Difficult emotions may rise again, but having navigated the prior wave, we're a bit more ready to take on the next one.

The pace and rhythm at which you ride the storm is up to you. Just focus on making it through today; don't worry about how you'll feel tomorrow. Each day gives you a chance to practice coping with your loss. Even though you may not feel brave in the moment, you are showing courage by facing your grief.

The storm may be strong, but so am I. And the shore is never out of reach.

SEPTEMBER 27

REPURPOSE YOUR PET'S ITEMS TO GROW A MEMORIAL PLANT. Consider upcycling your pet's food and water bowls to make planters. If you had reptiles or a small animal, consider repurposing their terrarium or vivarium into a desert plant garden. Aquariums can also be turned into terrariums and used for the same purpose. Filling these items with living, breathing plants is a way to continue the circle of life while keeping your pet's memory alive. Consider adding memorial stones to the décor.

From what once held their life, I nurture new life.

SEPTEMBER 28

"To invite a guest is to take the responsibility of his happiness during his stay under our roof."

—JEAN ANTHELME BRILLAT-SAVARIN

Some pets are excited to have new visitors in the home. Other pets are completely indifferent and still others hide or lunge when company arrives. This varies across species and among individuals. While you are grieving, you may hesitate to have people visit you, for fear it will bring back memories of your pet greeting visitors (or hiding from them). There is no need to force this process. When you are ready, pick somebody who is understanding and tell them your concerns before they visit. Start with a short one, perhaps for a cup of coffee. As you become more comfortable, you'll naturally resume a social cadence that works for you.

I can slowly welcome others back into my world.

SEPTEMBER 29

HOW DID YOUR PET REACT TO COMPANY? Think back to how your pet responded when someone came to visit. Maybe they greeted guests with excitement or curiosity—or perhaps they watched from a distance or approached others with extreme protectiveness for you and your family. Some pets are more selective, while others are exuberant. If your pet lived in a terrarium, cage, or aquarium, how did they respond when someone stood nearby? Share any lighthearted or memorable moments that capture their unique personality when someone new entered their space.

The threshold of our home is no longer the same without you. And still, your mischief and charm warm my heart.

SEPTEMBER 30

"But memory . . . Think how determinedly it entwines itself around the past!" —RONALD A. KNOX

Remembering all aspects of our pet's personality—what they looked like, sounded like, how they moved—can help keep them alive longer in our minds. Our mind briefly stores what we see, hear, smell, touch, and taste. It then sorts through the sensory details we've collected and moves those it deems significant to our long-term memory. Most people can combine the factual description of what happened, known as autobiographical memory, with images and sounds from that day, creating a recollection that plays like a movie in their mind.

There are many ways to still feel the presence of my beloved pet.

OCTOBER 1

WHAT DID YOUR PET ABSOLUTELY DISLIKE? Even the most agreeable pet has something they dislike. Many pets hate going to the vet. Others panic the moment the bathtub water starts running. Describe foods your pet refused to eat or smells they could not stand. If they had a funny way of turning things down, such as knocking over the food bowl or pushing your hand away, make sure to jot that down, too.

Remembering your quirks brings a smile to my face.

OCTOBER 2

**“Deep in the sun-searched growths the dragon-fly;
Hangs like a blue thread loosened from the sky.”**

—DANTE GABRIEL ROSSETTI

The dragonfly is a symbol of hope and renewal all around the world. It starts out as a nymph, living in the water and shedding its exoskeleton several times. When it reaches its final size, it emerges from the water and becomes a winged dragonfly. For many grieving individuals, a visit from a dragonfly is seen as a comforting message from their loved one. Others are hesitant to speak about anything they see as a sign or message from their pet. They are afraid they will be minimized or ridiculed. If you find comfort by interpreting something as a sign, that's all that matters. You do not owe anyone an explanation.

I am open to the many forms that solace may take.

OCTOBER 3

WHAT WOULD YOU CONSIDER A SIGN OR MESSAGE FROM YOUR PET? Some people find comfort in visits from cardinals, dragonflies, or butterflies. They may see a plant blossom that hasn't bloomed in a while or hear music they associate with their pet at important times. Consider cultural or religious traditions around signs and symbols. If you haven't had this experience, write about what sign would be the most meaningful to you.

Whether through signs, memories, or moments of stillness, our bond continues.

OCTOBER 4

"My best friend, she will always live on in my heart. Let's never take for granted the unconditional love that our animals show us every single day." —GISELE BÜNDCHEN

For many pet caregivers, part of the joy of having an animal companion is getting to share them with the world—through photos, funny stories, social media, or simply watching others fall in love with them, too. After a loss, that impulse doesn't necessarily disappear; it may just pause for a while, as you tend to your grief.

When you feel ready, continuing to talk about your pet can be a powerful act of remembrance. You're not only honoring their life, you're also allowing their legacy to ripple outward. Whether it's sharing a favorite photo, retelling a funny memory, or simply saying their name, you keep their light moving through the world.

In your honor, I keep sharing your light.

OCTOBER 5

MAKE A JOY LIST. Write down three to five moments when your pet brought joy to others and to you. This could be through a funny habit, a loving gesture, or simply their presence. This can include reactions from people to photos you posted on social media or to stories you told to others. They don't need to be dramatic. These are small, warm moments that made people smile, laugh, or feel comforted.

I remember you as a joy machine.

OCTOBER 6

"Give sorrow words." —WILLIAM SHAKESPEARE

Grief often leaves us speechless—not because the feelings aren't there, but because we don't always have the words for them. As you read more about grief at large, as well as pet grief, specifically, you will gain vocabulary to express your emotions. For example, people don't often use the word "yearning" in everyday conversation, but it can be a useful term to describe the deep, painful longing to reconnect with your pet. Most importantly, learning about grief and the words that encapsulate it can validate your experience and help you feel less alone.

In learning about grief, I explore a universal experience that helps me feel less alone.

OCTOBER 7

BUILD YOUR GRIEF VOCABULARY. Choose a word that reflects how you're feeling, such as "yearning," "guilt," or "devotion." Look up its definition, then describe what it means to you personally and how it shows up in your grief. Write a short recollection or reflection tied to that feeling. Repeat this with a few different words over the week. As your vocabulary grows, you may find it easier to understand and express your emotions—and feel less alone in them.

Words won't take the pain away, but they can help me carry it with more clarity.

OCTOBER 8

"It is said that time heals wounds. I don't agree. The wounds remain. The mind, protecting its sanity, covers them with some scar tissue and the pain lessens but it is never gone."

—ROSE FITZGERALD KENNEDY

Despite the popular adage that "time heals all wounds," the truth is that the pain of loss might always be there in some form. While the intensity of our grief can lessen, time isn't a magic wand that erases pain. The word "healed" implies that something is cured, that there is no sign of it anymore. But you don't "get over" losing a loved one. Grieving is a process you go through to adapt to that loss. Time alone doesn't fix grief, but it can give you the space and distance needed to better cope with it.

I'm not looking for a cure for my grief, I am looking for the skills to manage it.

OCTOBER 9

TAKE A MINDFUL WALK. Mindful walking is a simple exercise to root you in the present moment. Choose comfortable clothing and a relaxing route. While you are walking, note all the sensations in your body. Note the feeling of your feet on the ground, your legs as they move, and your breath. Note what you observe in your surroundings. If you feel ready for it, imagine your pet is with you and talk to them about what you observe. If walking isn't available to you, sit outside and take note of each of your senses: What do you see, hear, smell, taste? What do you feel on your face?

I trust in the soothing properties of my natural surroundings.

OCTOBER 10

“I know that music is the most healing thing in the world.”

—ALICIA KEYS

Grief can leave the world feeling heavy and disjointed, but there are moments, however brief, when something within us begins to hum again. The “music” we hear may not be a melody, but a feeling of emotional alignment or inner harmony. These moments might come through stillness, creativity, connection, or recollection. They are not a sign that grief is over, but rather that healing is quietly at work. Whether or not you play an instrument or sing, tuning in to what helps restore that internal rhythm can offer comfort and ease.

I can find ways to lift my heart even as it aches.

OCTOBER 11

MAKE TIME TO LISTEN TO MUSIC. Music often bypasses the thinking mind and speaks directly to the heart, offering release and comfort. This week, schedule a listening party for yourself. It can be any length of time with any musical genre. Include old favorites that remind you of your pet or try something entirely new. Add some movement or sing along if it feels right. Let the music meet you where you are.

In music, I find a safe place for my feelings to rise and flow.

OCTOBER 12

"For me, knitting is a release. It lets my hands lead the way as my mind trails behind . . . I truly believe that when you know you are capable of small tasks, it makes the bigger ones feel easier." —MICHELLE OBAMA

Learning a new hobby, or picking an old one back up, can be a therapeutic part of the grieving process. It gives you something meaningful to focus on and can help fill the time once spent with your pet. It can also help establish new routines and engage new people or animals. Many activities, like gardening, cake decorating, or playing video games, encourage mindfulness by drawing your attention to the present moment. Others, especially those with repetitive motions like knitting or running, allow your mind to wander and process emotions more freely. Hobbies come in many forms: active (like pickleball or hiking), creative (arts and crafts, writing), social (affinity clubs), or cerebral (puzzles and games). In trying something new, you may discover fulfillment in an unexpected place.

It's okay to let the present moment distract me from thoughts of the past. Everyone needs moments of reprieve.

OCTOBER 13

TRY A NEW HOBBY. When you're grieving, it's easy to lose touch with parts of yourself that once felt vibrant or curious. Hobbies can help you reconnect to those parts. Consider starting a hobby this week or picking up an old one that you haven't done for a while. You can start by doing an online search for "hobby ideas," then look for stores, clubs, or classes in your area. If you belong to a community center, consider looking for classes and activities there. Maybe you have a friend or acquaintance who you know engages in a hobby that interests you. Ask if they can tell you what they enjoy about it and perhaps show you some of the basics. If you feel like connecting with strangers, there are many apps to help you find hiking, language-practice, or dance groups—among many others—in your area.

I start by engaging with small activities that give me comfort.

OCTOBER 14

**"Spun of all silks, our days and nights
Have sorrows woven with delights."**

—FRANÇOIS DE MALHERBE

Grief experts emphasize the importance of expressing the thoughts and feelings that accompany loss and coming to terms with the reality of their loss but it's okay—essential even—to take breaks. Dr. M. Katherine Shear of Columbia University explains that, at first, "The emotional pain associated with new information that a loved one has died is so severe that people need time interspersed with periods of respite in order to be able to fully acknowledge the unwanted reality."

As the person gradually integrates the reality of the loss, they no longer need to avoid the triggers or thoughts that previously caused severe pain. Respite activities can include self-care such as getting a massage or eating a healthy meal. You can also focus on generating positive emotions through engaging in enjoyable activities—even five minutes counts—and focusing your mind on neutral or pleasant thoughts.

I allow myself respite from my grief.

OCTOBER 15

TAKE A NIGHTTIME BATH OR SHOWER TO RELAX. A relaxing shower or bath before bedtime is a healthy way to calm your nervous system. For a bath, consider using your favorite bubbles or bath salts. If you have achy muscles, you can try Epsom salts. Add some music or relaxing environmental sounds. For the shower, use your favorite body wash and scrubber to exfoliate. Make sure to lotion up after your shower and put on fresh pajamas. Top it off with a cup of chamomile tea.

Acts of relaxation, quite literally, replenish my cells.

OCTOBER 16

"Uncertainty is the refuge of hope." —HENRI FRÉDÉRIC AMIEL

It's hard to predict a grief reaction. Each person grieves differently, and each loss will be experienced differently. That's why there are no "shoulds" in grief. If your reaction is different from what you expected, you may be feeling anxious and uncertain about what is going to happen next. Learning to tolerate uncertainty can reduce your anxiety in the long run, and you can make room for hope that whatever happens, you'll manage it.

There's no map for this grief journey. I will travel it one step at a time.

OCTOBER 17

WRITE A LETTER TO YOUR PAST SELF. If you could go back in time, what advice would you give your past self about your grief experience? How close were your predictions about what this would feel like? What words of comfort could you offer to prepare yourself for the loss to come? If you'd like, write this down in the form of a letter, seal it in an envelope, and read it one year from now. See if your advice has changed.

I learn and grow from each new experience.

OCTOBER 18

"Ah, woe is me! Winter is come and gone, But grief returns with the revolving year." —PERCY BYSSHE SHELLEY

During the year that follows a loss, you may experience several difficult "firsts." There will be birthdays and holidays without your beloved pet. There will be anniversaries of different milestones in your life. For some, the second year can be even harder because you may not be expecting a resurgence of grief. Externally, others may have assumed you "moved on." It's important to acknowledge that these moments are hard, and that doesn't mean you're moving backward. It means you loved deeply. As these dates approach, consider preparing for them. That could mean creating space to honor your feelings, planning something meaningful, or reaching out for extra support.

Thank you for making the special days so special.

OCTOBER 19

MARK YOUR CALENDAR FOR DATES WHERE YOU MIGHT NEED EXTRA SUPPORT. Think about holidays, your birthday, your pet's birthday, and other significant times of the year. In your calendar, mark a few days ahead of that date as a "preparation day." You can set reminders on your phone if it helps. Make sure that you have support numbers handy. Discuss the day ahead of time with friends or in any online groups you may be a part of. The night before, engage in self-care activities you find relaxing or that can provide a mental respite.

Planning ahead can help me manage resurgences of grief in ways that work for me.

OCTOBER 20

"We can not hinder the birds of sorrow from flying over our head, but we can prevent them from building a nest in our hair." —MARTIN LUTHER

Grief therapy involves short-term, specialized counseling to help you process loss. There are many reasons you may want to seek out this specific type of therapy. You and your pet may have experienced a trauma that resulted in their death, such as a fire or natural disaster. You may be experiencing ambiguous grief and can't cope with the uncertainty of not knowing where your pet is. You may have grief symptoms that have impacted your functioning for more than one year. Your grief may have intensified existing anxiety, depression, or PTSD. You may have limited social support and don't feel comfortable attending a support group. Whatever the reason, there is no shame in reaching out for help. Everyone needs extra support in difficult emotional times.

Asking for help is not a sign of weakness. It's a sign that I'm ready to heal.

OCTOBER 21

TIPS ON FINDING A THERAPIST: There are many licensed therapists who specialize in grief, some of whom are specially trained in pet bereavement. If you are already seeing a therapist, you can ask if they also do grief therapy and if not, if they can refer you to a specialist. To find a pet bereavement specialist, you can call your veterinarian's office or any local veterinary hospital and ask if they can refer you to a veterinary social worker. You can also ask for a referral from pet bereavement groups and support hotlines. For more resources, see Support Groups and Counseling in the appendix.

I am open to support so I can continue to flourish in this one precious life.

OCTOBER 22

"We cannot destroy kindred: our chains stretch a little sometimes, but they never break."

—MARIE DE RABUTIN-CHANTAL, MARQUISE DE SÉVIGNÉ

Because your pet was part of the family, they may have played a role in maintaining harmony in the home. In some families, a pet can act as a buffer between people and prevent conflict. For partners, the pet may have kept one person company while the other was away from home for long periods of time. After pet loss, it can be a stressful adjustment for the family or partners. It's important to talk about what's happening and look for solutions together. For example, if your partner is away often, you can schedule more frequent check-ins while they are traveling or working. Or if taking care of your pet gave your child structure and fewer behavioral problems, you can identify new responsibilities for them to take on, such as caring for the plants in the home.

It is okay if it takes time for our family to adjust to this loss.

OCTOBER 23

SCHEDULE A FAMILY MEETING OR A TALK WITH YOUR PARTNER. Do this only if everyone feels ready to have a discussion. Start with each person sharing how they feel, and what needs are not being met. Make sure everyone else uses active listening—not interrupting and acknowledging what the other person is saying. See if you can come up with an action plan on how to better support each other.

It is an act of love to listen.

OCTOBER 24

"Parting is all we know of heaven,
And all we need of hell." —EMILY DICKINSON

When your pet dies, it may seem like a lot of pets are suddenly dying, too. This may be for more than one reason. If your pet had a chronic or long-term illness, you may have joined caregiver groups or met people at the veterinary hospital whose pets were also ill. You may hear about the deaths of those animals more often because you knew so many with terminal illnesses.

Another explanation is that your brain may be paying more attention to news about pet loss because you have recently lost a pet. There's even a name for it: the Baader–Meinhof phenomenon, also known as frequency illusion. This cognitive bias can make your grief feel even more expansive. Understanding why it *seems* like so many animal companions are dying can help relieve some of those feelings of overwhelm.

Giving myself a break from negative emotions doesn't mean I love my pet any less.

OCTOBER 25

HAVE A STRICTLY POSITIVE MEDIA DAY. Set aside one day this week to only view content that's positive and uplifting. Steer clear of the news. No sad movies. No true crime podcasts. No distressing documentaries. If you're a reader, stick to reading humorous or inspirational books or articles. Try to get outside. Jot down notes at the end of the day about how you feel after consuming strictly positive content. If you enjoy this activity, plan another day like this one.

In viewing uplifting stories, I begin to see the light in my own life. In other words: hope.

OCTOBER 26

"The rawness I have felt over these past few days and sleepless nights at the idea of my little man being lost and scared, with me unable to do anything to protect him, is a waking nightmare."

—ORLANDO BLOOM, ABOUT HIS LATE DOG, MIGHTY

One of the most harrowing experiences a caregiver can go through is *ambiguous grief*, the terrifying experience of not knowing if your loved one is dead or alive, or suffering in any way. This can happen if your pet runs away, is stolen, or is caught up in a natural disaster, really any experience where there is an unknown factor.

I briefly experienced ambiguous grief on 9/11. I was in Los Angeles on business but lived near the World Trade Center and had boarded my cat, Sugar Ray, a few blocks away. I could not get through to the boarding facility for 48 hours and was completely frantic. Was he alive? Was he all alone and frightened? Hungry? It wasn't until two days later that the manager was able to email me, letting me know Sugar Ray was safe. I'm sure you can imagine how tightly I hugged my brave boy when we were reunited. This experience only lasted a few days. For others, ambiguous grief can be open-ended. If this is you, it's helpful to acknowledge that your grief is as valid as any other type of grief.

There are many types of grief and all of them are valid.

OCTOBER 27

REDUCE STRESS BY ATTENDING A MEDITATION OR YOGA CLASS. When you don't feel like talking, you can revel in the calm silence of a meditation or yoga class. Both meditation and yoga reduce stress by lowering cortisol levels, heart rate, and blood pressure. They can pull you into the present moment when you're overwhelmed with thoughts of the future or past. If you want company, check the schedules of studios near you for in-person classes. Most studios have classes for every level of practitioner, including chair yoga for seniors or people with limited mobility. If you prefer to practice alone, or if you're not feeling motivated to leave the house, you can find meditation and yoga videos for free online.

I don't need to have the right words. In this moment, I offer myself quiet care.

OCTOBER 28

**"Alas, I have grieved so I am hard to love.
Yet love me—wilt thou? Open thine heart wide."**

—ELIZABETH BARRETT BROWNING

Grief can change how we relate to others. You may feel withdrawn, numb, or overwhelmed—so much so that even the people you love most feel far away. Or you may crave closeness, longing for connection and comfort. Both responses are valid. The truth is, grief can make it difficult to know what you need moment to moment, and it can be just as hard for others to know how to support you.

The people who care about you may not always say or do the perfect thing, but their presence, if offered with patience and compassion, is a gift. If you need space, that is also a form of honesty and self-care. Letting others love you through your grief is one way the healing begins.

I can open my heart when I want to and set limits when I need to.

OCTOBER 29

REACH OUT TO SOMEONE TODAY TO LET THEM KNOW YOU ARE PROCESSING YOUR GRIEF. Consider sending an email, text, or handwritten note to someone you are thinking about. Let them know that you may not have the capacity to spend a lot of time with them, but that you appreciate them. I had a client, Ted, who told me he felt terrible, because an old buddy had reached out to him months prior, and he was embarrassed that he hadn't responded. "The longer I wait, the harder it gets to even text him," he said.

I asked him, "What's the worst that can happen if you text him?" He replied, "He might be really angry with me, and ghost me." Then I asked him, "Have you seen him behave like this with you or anyone else before?"

He smiled and said, "Never. He's an understanding guy, so I bet he'll be relieved, not angry." He sent the text he had already written, and the following session he told me that they had dinner and caught up. If there are people who've reached out but who you haven't felt ready to respond to, let them know you're okay and that you still want them to check in from time to time. This will reassure them and keep you connected. There is no timeline you need to adhere to.

True friends are understanding and compassionate.

OCTOBER 30

"You will forever be my little angel, forever missed, and forever loved. You may be physically gone, but the imprint of your pawprints on my life will never fade." —PARIS HILTON

Paris Hilton's dogs are almost as famous as she is, often accessorized as stylishly as the heiress. But our pets don't have to have a famous mom to be superstars. When I miss my sweet cat, Joni, I love looking at a series of photos I took of her when I caught her playing with a feather boa I had worn on Halloween. Maybe there was a time when you said, "Wait, hold that pose!" as you grabbed your phone to capture a similar fabulous moment. Looking back at those photos, when you're ready, can help you feel close to your own beloved.

It's possible that my memories with you become more vivid with time. I will never forget you.

OCTOBER 31

MAKE A COLLAGE OF YOUR PET'S GLAMOUR PHOTOS. Find photos of your pet's best looks. They can be funny or glamourous, hamming it up or auspiciously demure.

As I embrace your "goofy" side, I feel emboldened to be the truest version of myself.

NOVEMBER 1

"There are moments in life, which are never forgot[ten], which brighten, and brighten, as time steals away."

—JAMES GATES PERCIVAL

While some memories fade, others become brighter over time. Special events or holidays, especially those dedicated to remembrance, can help us honor and enliven these memories. My client Sandra included her beloved dog, Max, in her family's celebration of Day of the Dead ("Dia de los Muertos"), a Mexican holiday that honors the spirit of loved ones who've departed with altars ("ofrendas")—adorned with photos, favorite foods, drinks, and belongings. Sandra created an ofrenda for her sweet Max with photos and her favorite toys and treats. In addition to being healing, the ritual spotlighted memories that will live with her forever.

You live on, curled up in a special place in my heart.

NOVEMBER 2

WRITE ABOUT A SPECIAL DAY WITH YOUR PET. This day could be a birthday, a holiday, or any special day. Describe the location where you spent the day, what the weather was like, who was with you, and what activities you and your pet enjoyed. Try to paint a picture of this day with your words, to help brighten the memory.

In recording our memories, our story lives on.

NOVEMBER 3

". . . The practice of medicine is an art, not a trade; a calling, not a business; a calling in which your heart will be exercised equally with your head." —SIR WILLIAM OSLER

Though Sir William Osler was a pioneering physician, his words resonate far beyond human medicine. They speak to the emotional depth and dedication of all who care for others, especially those who devote their lives to the well-being of animals.

This calling is not limited to veterinarians and veterinary technicians. Anyone who loves and cares for animals knows that compassion is central to this work. The bonds we form with animals are real, deep, and lasting. And when we lose them, it hurts. If you are someone who has poured your heart into caring for a pet—your own or someone else's—remember to offer yourself the same compassion and tenderness you would give to others in grief.

Thank you for letting me care for you.

NOVEMBER 4

HOW AND WHEN DID YOU DEVELOP A LOVE FOR ANIMALS? Think about your earliest interest in animals. Maybe it was spurred by a wildlife documentary you saw, a book you read, interactions with family pets, livestock, or neighborhood animals. If you work in the veterinary field, what inspired you to enter the profession? What made you want to care for animals for a living? Consider sharing your story with a friend, an online group, or in your journal.

My love for animals is a meaningful part of who I am.

NOVEMBER 5

"A good deed is never lost; he who sows courtesy reaps friendship, and he who plants kindness gathers love." —SAINT BASIL

Animals show us, in quiet and profound ways, what it means to live in service of love. Service animals exemplify this with extraordinary dedication. They are trained to assist with daily tasks, provide emotional grounding, and often save lives. The bond between a person and their service animal is uniquely close, built on constant companionship, trust, and mutual reliance. Losing that presence can feel like losing a part of oneself.

But the power of the human-animal bond isn't limited to service animals. Many of us have known animals who offered emotional support simply by being themselves—through companionship, affection, protection, or silent presence during difficult times. Whether they were trained to help or just instinctively knew when we needed comfort, their kindness leaves a lasting imprint.

Your lightness and care made me feel seen.

NOVEMBER 6

TIPS FOR ADJUSTING TO A NEW ANIMAL. Sometimes we have a new animal enter our lives before we feel ready. This can happen if you need a service animal or if you are outnumbered in the family's choice to get a new pet. One thing you can do is to continue to speak about your pet to the successor animal if that feels right to you. Some people like to refer to their pet as the successor's "big brother" or "big sister." If your family members insisted on getting a new pet before you were ready, build up to interacting with them at a pace that feels comfortable. Remember, you are not betraying the pet you have lost by building a relationship with their successor.

I can hold space for grief and new beginnings at the same time.

NOVEMBER 7

"Thou art gone from my gaze like a beautiful dream, and I seek thee in vain by the meadow and stream." —GEORGE LINLEY

Yearning is a feeling most people experience after a loss. It is sometimes described as so painful that the body physically aches; other times it's a bittersweet mix of fond memories and sad nostalgia. You might catch yourself thinking, "I just want my pet back," or "I wish things would go back to the way they were before they died." It is a rational impulse to idealize the past when the present feels dark and heavy. As with grief, yearning is unique to each individual and may change throughout the course of your grieving process. However it shows up for you, know that yearning is a natural part of loving deeply and losing deeply.

I accept that my life has changed. My bond with you is still strong, but in a different form.

NOVEMBER 8

KEEP A CREDIT LIST TO BUILD SELF-CONFIDENCE. One way to break through the cycle of yearning and adapt to your loss is to do small things every day that give you a feeling of accomplishment. Every day this week, write down at least two things that you have accomplished. Make sure to give yourself accolades for each completed task, preferably out loud. You can include even the simplest assignment, like getting out of bed in the morning or washing your face. The important thing is to build self-confidence by acknowledging your progress. At the end of the week, review your list once more.

I don't have to stop grieving before I ease back into the rhythm of my life.

NOVEMBER 9

"Ah! there is nothing like staying at home for real comfort."

—JANE AUSTEN

Grieving can make it especially hard to navigate social events, work parties, and family gatherings. You may have already said "yes" to invitations or commitments before your loss that now feel overwhelming.

If you're not up for being social or pretending everything is okay, it's more than acceptable to step back. Politely declining or rescheduling is a form of self-care. You deserve space to process your emotions without pressure to perform or explain.

I may need to step back to keep myself standing.

NOVEMBER 10

PLAN AHEAD FOR THE END-OF-YEAR SOCIAL SEASON. Take a look at your calendar and identify what events you have coming up in the next few months. Identify any obligations that you want to skip. Reach out to the host ahead of time and let them know you won't be attending. Share as much or as little as you want about how you are feeling emotionally.

I am not obligated to accept every (or any!) invitations.

NOVEMBER 11

"It is while you are patiently toiling at the little tasks of life that the meaning and shape of the great whole of life dawns upon you." —PHILLIPS BROOKS

Grief counselor Lois Tonkin developed a model of grief that emphasizes "growing around grief." Tonkin based her model on a client who, after losing her child, was surprised to find that her grief did not shrink; her life simply grew around it. While she deeply grieved the loss of her child, she—eventually—engaged in new relationships and activities. According to Tonkin, there is comfort in knowing that you can coexist with your grief while experiencing personal growth.

In this loss, I find pockets of growth.

NOVEMBER 12

DRAW AN IMAGE OF GROWING AROUND GRIEF. Start with a circle that represents your grief. Go ahead and shade that in. Then draw a larger circle around your grief. Start filling it in with different activities you might like to try, or people you might like to visit, when you're ready. Include any places you might like to see. If you prefer, just think about a few easy activities you can do in the next few weeks.

My grief may get smaller as my life gets bigger, but the loss will always be part of who I am.

NOVEMBER 13

"Everybody needs beauty as well as bread, places to play in and pray in, where Nature may heal and cheer and give strength to body and soul alike." —JOHN MUIR

Research indicates spending time in nature improves mental well-being. This doesn't mean that you have to live in a forest or by the seaside. Taking a walk in a city park or sitting on a balcony to listen to birds can bring a sense of contentment and ease. Grieving can be an isolating experience, especially when we lose a pet, but time in nature offers a sense of connectedness with ourselves and the world at large.

I can turn to nature as a source of serenity and strength.

NOVEMBER 14

FIND RESPITE IN NATURE. Go for a walk in the woods or a nearby park if you are in a city. Spend some time in a garden, visit a botanical center, or browse a flower shop. Go for a drive somewhere you find mesmerizing. Take time to be present with the sensations of nature: breathing in the fresh air, listening to the sounds of rustling leaves, observing the texture of clouds, or welcoming the rush of the tide. If going outside is difficult for any reason, consider looking at photos or videos of the natural world.

Like my grief, the natural world is a place of both wildness and peace, new growth, and continual repair.

NOVEMBER 15

"A pleasant companion on a journey is as good as a carriage."

—PUBLILIUS SYRUS

Many caregivers enjoy traveling with their pets, whether by car, train, or plane. You may have fond memories of seeing them enjoying new environments and activities. If your pet spent most of their time at home, you may have kept in contact with them by observing them on a pet or house camera. It may feel lonely traveling without them by your side, and you might miss spying on them to see what mischief they'd get into while you were away. Find comfort knowing that your memories of them will go with you everywhere you go.

There is so much in this world for me to still discover. I look forward to you discovering it with me, tucked comfortably in my heart.

NOVEMBER 16

TIPS FOR TRAVELING AFTER PET LOSS: If you plan to travel anytime soon, consider carrying a memorial item with you. You can bring along a photo, keepsake, or article that belonged to them. (Because items can be lost or stolen while traveling, try to leave the most precious ones at home.) As with any memory, talking or writing about your travels together—even writing them a postcard while on your upcoming journeys—can help you feel connected to your pet.

NOVEMBER 17

"I loved my friend.
He went away from me. There's nothing more to say.
The poem ends, Soft as it began,— I loved my friend."

—LANGSTON HUGHES

This quote gets to the heart of losing a pet: Our best friend is gone. It's that simple. For many of us, there really is nothing more to say, nothing more to explain. The human-animal bond defies words, and it is difficult to explain what that's like to anyone who has not experienced it. What is clear to us is that we loved our friend. And that love is eternal.

Thank you for your friendship. It is one of the most meaningful connections of my life.

NOVEMBER 18

MAKE A MEMORIAL QUILT OR PILLOW FOR YOUR PET. If you have extra blankets or clothing from your pet, you can create a small blanket, pillowcase, or even a stuffed animal from the material. If you don't feel like sewing, consider cutting out some fabric from one of these items, perhaps in the shape of a heart, and using it as a patch for jeans or a jacket. If you don't feel like making something, simply fill an empty pillowcase with several items.

Love doesn't disappear; it transforms.

NOVEMBER 19

"Life is made up, not of great sacrifices or duties, but of little things, in which smiles and kindness, and small obligations, given habitually, are what win and preserve the heart, and secure comfort." —SIR HUMPHRY DAVY

In the wake of loss, it's often the small things that begin to bring light back into our lives—a warm cup of tea, a walk at dusk, the soft memory of your pet's favorite spot on the couch. Sometimes, the most profound response to loss is simply a quiet promise to live more intentionally, to cherish those we love while we can, and to notice the beauty in ordinary moments.

I take a moment to notice the magic in life's small moments.

NOVEMBER 20

SMALL THINGS, OFTEN. Choose one small, comforting ritual to incorporate into your day—something simple that helps you pause and reconnect. This could be lighting a candle in the evening, taking a short walk at the same time each day, or sitting quietly with a warm drink while watching the sky. As you do it, gently recall a fond memory of your pet or offer a quiet thank-you for the love you shared. Let this moment be a touchstone, a way to honor the past while grounding yourself in the present.

Each ritual is a thread that connects me to you.

NOVEMBER 21

"The fall of a leaf is a whisper to the living." —RUSSIAN PROVERB

Tucked away in New York City's Central Park, there once stood an 18-foot tree bearing much more than leaves. Every year in late November, this tree blossomed with heartfelt tributes to beloved animals who had passed away. The secret holiday tradition of decorating what was known as the Furever Tree started in 1986 and lasted until 2024. The laminated photos and handwritten tributes that hung from the tree numbered close to 2,000. They were painstakingly preserved every year by two volunteers who kept them in storage and took them out to decorate the tree—a testament to the deep and enduring love we caregivers have for our beloved pets.

Hushed moments of reflection can carry deep meaning for those who are paying attention.

NOVEMBER 22

HONOR THE MEMORY OF YOUR PET THIS SEASON. This could be as simple as hanging a favorite photo on a wall, placing a keepsake on a shelf, or writing their name on a paper leaf and taping it to a window or mirror. If you're decorating for a holiday, consider adding an ornament or ribbon in their memory. You might also include tributes to other animals who've touched your life—real or fictional, near or far. These small acts of remembrance are quiet whispers that love continues on.

Each small tribute says: You are remembered, you are cherished, and you are always part of my story.

NOVEMBER 23

"There is no despair so absolute as that which comes with the first moments of our first great sorrow, when we have not yet known what it is to have suffered and be healed, to have despaired and have recovered hope." —GEORGE ELIOT

The first time you experience a significant loss can be scary and stressful. You may be feeling emotions—such as longing, sorrow, or emptiness—that are new or far deeper than anything you've known before. Even if you've grieved in the past, this moment can feel unfamiliar, because every loss touches a different part of your heart. It may seem like you'll never feel "normal" again, and that can be overwhelming. But just as sorrow is new, so too is the resilience that slowly begins to form in its wake.

I honor the depth of my sorrow without rushing my healing. Though this pain is new, I trust that with time, love, and care, I will find my way forward.

NOVEMBER 24

TRY PROGRESSIVE MUSCLE RELAXATION TO DE-STRESS. Grief, especially in the first few days and weeks—or when experiencing it for the first time—can be extremely stressful. Progressive muscle relaxation (PMR) is a technique to de-stress by tensing and then relaxing muscle groups from head to toe. Here's how it works:

1. Find a comfortable position and take three deep breaths.
2. Inhale, scrunch up your toes, then relax your muscles while you exhale.
3. Repeat, but this time tense both your calves.
4. Repeat with each muscle group moving upward: thighs and buttocks; abdomen; arms and hands; shoulders and back; and finally, your face (scrunch up your eyes and smile).

This exercise should take about 5–10 minutes to complete. When you are done, you should feel deeply relaxed. Use PMR before bedtime to help you sleep.

With each breath and gentle release, I invite calm into my body.

"We all have in our hearts a secret place where we keep, free from the contact of the world, our sweetest remembrances."

—J. DE FINOD

NOVEMBER 25

Sharing memories with others is a meaningful and healing part of grief. But there's also something sacred about holding certain memories close—like sharing a secret with a best friend or writing in a diary tucked safely away. These private moments can be deeply comforting, reminding us of the quiet, personal bond we shared with our pet. When you revisit those memories in solitude, imagine your pet beside you, sharing in the warmth and joy of that moment once more.

Every fond memory is a moment of love I give myself. In remembering, I feel connected, comforted, and never truly alone.

NOVEMBER 26

SET ASIDE SOME TIME TO REMINISCE. This week, set aside 10 or 15 minutes to simply sit quietly and reminisce. Try to retrieve memories that you haven't thought of in a while. Maybe it was a toy they played with a few years ago or something you did together that was a switch from your usual routine. Imagine your pet is with you and say, "Remember that time when you ____?" Keep track of any memory that makes you smile. Make a note of it so you can think of it again when you are feeling blue.

I am learning to tolerate the pain of grief, so I can get to the joy of reminiscing about you.

NOVEMBER 27

"Let our lives be pure as snow-fields, where our footsteps leave a mark, but not a stain." —MADAME SWETCHINE

One of the things we love most about our pets is their pure-hearted presence: their innocence, loyalty, and the unconditional love they so freely give. They move through the world without judgment, leaving behind warmth, companionship, and joy. Whether through quiet comfort, playful energy, or their ability to sense when we need them most, animals often make the world better simply by being in it. Their time with us, though too brief, leaves a lasting impression. In their simplicity, they teach us something profound: to live with kindness, to be present, and to love without condition.

In the simplicity of your love, I learned the art of living.

NOVEMBER 28

CELEBRATE THE DAY OF YOUR PET'S PASSING. Many people choose to honor their beloved companion by marking the day they passed as their *angelversary*. There are many meaningful ways to observe this day. You might perform an act of kindness in their memory or gather with close friends or family to share stories, look at photos, and celebrate the love you shared. Some people visit a place their pet loved or one they had hoped to go to together. If it's the first anniversary and you're not ready for a memorial, that's okay. Consider doing something calming or restorative just for yourself. This day is about love, not pressure. Honoring your grief in whatever form it takes is more than enough.

Today, I remember with love. Whether through action or stillness, I honor the bond we shared.

NOVEMBER 29

"Kindness to animals is no unworthy exercise of benevolence . . . The inevitable shortness then of their existence should plead for them touchingly." —SIR ARTHUR HELPS

Time with our pets is precious and fleeting, which makes small acts of kindness all the more powerful. Whether you're a longtime pet parent, a foster caregiver, a shelter volunteer, or someone who simply offered love to a neighborhood animal, your care mattered. The bond you formed, no matter how long or brief, is worthy of grief, reflection, and remembrance.

Caring for animals, especially in challenging settings like shelters, can come with great emotional weight. You may be carrying the memory of an animal you only knew for a short while, or one who was never officially "yours," but touched your heart deeply. Whether you continue to care for animals or simply honor the one you've lost, your kindness is part of a legacy that lives on.

Every act of care is meaningful.

NOVEMBER 30

BRING TREATS TO THE NEAREST SHELTER. Most shelters and rescues need supplies and appreciate even small gifts. Consider dropping off some snacks (unopened) or a few toys. Call ahead or check the shelter's website or "wish list" to see what they need. If allowed, consider bringing treats or coffee for the shelter workers. They deserve our gratitude. This is also a way to honor your own role as a caregiver for your pet.

I am thankful for all the people around the world who love and care for animals.

DECEMBER 1

"What is life? It is a flash of a firefly in the night. It is a breath of a buffalo in the winter time. It is as the little shadow that runs across the grass and loses itself in the sunset."

—CHIEF CROWFOOT, CHIEF OF THE SIKSIKA NATION

As you look back on the precious time you spent with your pet, it may seem like it went by so quickly. Whether you had one month or 20 years together, it may feel to you like that time passed too quickly. Grief may change how you value time going forward. Some people find they are more motivated to engage in new activities or show gratitude to loved ones more frequently. Do what feels right for you and only when you are ready.

Loss is a reminder of everything I still have.

DECEMBER 2

IF YOU WERE GIVEN 24 HOURS TO SPEND WITH YOUR PET, WHAT WOULD YOU DO? If you feel ready, picture your pet healthy and at whatever age you choose. Describe where you would go and what you would do together. What would you say to them—and what might they say back to you? (Since this is a daydream, let them talk!)

This imaginative exercise can be deeply comforting during grief. It offers a safe space to revisit joy, express love, and even say things that were left unsaid. By visualizing your continued bond, you can soften the sharp edges of loss and feel connected to your pet in a new way. If this brings you comfort, know you can return to them anytime, simply by closing your eyes and imagining it all again.

I cherish every second I spent with you.

DECEMBER 3

"Grief divided is made lighter." —PROVERB

Many people refer to their pet as their "baby" and to themselves as a pet parent. If you're a pet parent, then your parents might refer to themselves as your pet's grandparents. Just like with human children, many pets love being spoiled by their grandparents. Your friends and family members may have taken care of your pet when you were away, acting as doting loved ones. If your pet had meaningful relationships with other humans, then there's a chance they are grieving, too. Reaching out to them can help all of you process this grief.

As we remember together, we heal together.

DECEMBER 4

REACH OUT TO YOUR PET'S EXTENDED FAMILY. Think of other humans who grew close to your baby. A neighbor, a pet-sitter or dogwalker, even just a friend who loved to play with them when they visited. They may be feeling the loss, too. When you feel ready, reach out to them. You can send a text or make a phone call. You can also send a card or a handwritten note that includes a photo of your pet for them to have as a keepsake. If you're up for company, consider inviting them over. You can help each other through the grief.

My pet was loved by many, and that love continues even in their absence.

DECEMBER 5

"A feeling of sadness and longing,
That is not akin to pain, And resembles sorrow only
As the mist resembles the rain."

—HENRY WADSWORTH LONGFELLOW

Grief doesn't always arrive in obvious ways. Sometimes it's a sharp ache, and other times it's a longing that drifts in softly, like mist that's hard to define but still deeply felt. Sorrow can take many forms, and each is valid.

The intensity of grief varies from person to person, and for each person it may change from day to day, even hour to hour. In whatever way it shows up for you—heavy or light, distant or raw—it matters. You deserve to feel supported through it all. Allow yourself to move through these emotions without judgment. There's no right way to grieve, only your way.

I allow myself to experience grief in whatever form it takes, with patience and without judgment.

DECEMBER 6

TAKE MOMENTS TO SEPARATE FROM YOUR GRIEF. At times, it may be easier to process your grief by thinking of it as a separate entity. We can do this with a simple visualization. Imagine your grief as a separate person, pocket-sized, that you carry around with you. Some days they might be crying, other days they might be in pain. What does this little person look like? What do they sound like? How are they feeling today? Speak to them with words of comfort. Check in with them throughout the day.

I can sit beside my grief without becoming it. With compassion and curiosity, I listen to what it needs.

DECEMBER 7

"Life is a flower of which Love is its honey." —VICTOR HUGO

Life gives us the opportunity to experience the sweetness of love. Our pets offer unconditional love and, in turn, eagerly receive love from us. When you grieve their loss, you're missing not only their presence but also that mutual exchange of affection—a bond woven through shared routines, quiet moments, and wordless understanding.

At some point, you may consider opening your heart to another companion animal—but that decision is deeply personal, and there is no timeline or obligation. If and when you do, it's helpful to remember that each animal is unique. I've had clients surprised by the demands of an exuberant young animal because they were used to the gentle, elderly one who passed away. It can be helpful to remember what your pet was like when they were an untrained ball of energy and give yourself time to build a new rhythm. Whether or not you choose to bring another animal into your life, the love you shared remains real, lasting, and yours to carry forward.

What a miracle that we crossed paths in this lifetime.

DECEMBER 8

HOW DID YOU BUILD YOUR RELATIONSHIP WITH YOUR PET? Think about your early days together. Was it love at first sight, or did it take some time to feel a meaningful connection? Did your pet need any kind of training? Try to recall a specific moment when you felt close to them for the first time.

To think—how I loved you in those early days. And our love only grew.

DECEMBER 9

"My heart is wax to be moulded as she pleases but enduring as marble to retain." —MIGUEL DE CERVANTES

Visualizing our hearts as wax makes so much sense in the context of our relationship to pets. We soften our hearts to let them in and just like a wax mold—their paws leave a lasting imprint. They offer us so much warmth that in moments of utter cuteness we feel our hearts "melt" like wax for them. The impression that beloved pets leave behind is solid and enduring. In their own way, they help us into the people we become.

I am grateful for the softness you brought to my heart.

DECEMBER 10

TEND TO THE IMPRINT THEY LEFT BEHIND. Take time today to nurture the soft place in your heart where your pet left their mark. Revisit a memory that warms you, maybe a quirky habit, a moment of unexpected comfort, or the way they greeted you after a long day. If it feels right, watch a short video or read a story about animals who've overcome hardship, reminding yourself of the resilience and joy that animals bring into the world. You might even light a candle or hold a keepsake while you do this, a small representation of the warmth they gave you. Think of this as caring for the soft spot in your heart where your pet still rests, curled up in the imprint only they could make.

I take moments today to notice and nurture the warmth in my heart.

DECEMBER 11

"There is a certain pleasure in weeping; grief is soothed and alleviated by tears." —OVID

Tears can be healing, but they don't always come when we expect or want them to. When my mother passed away, it took several weeks before I was able to fully cry. I desperately wanted my tears to flow, but I couldn't access them. Then one day, during an acting class exercise about meaningful experiences, I spoke about my mom. As I shared her memory, the tears finally came. In that moment, something softened. A weight lifted, and from then on, I was more able to access the grief that had been quietly building inside me.

You may have had, or will have, a moment like this—when something unlocks the tears and helps grief move through you. Whether your release comes through conversation, art, nature, or stillness, trust that it's your body's way of beginning to heal.

I can allow myself to release this grief.

DECEMBER 12

WATCH OR READ SOMETHING THAT WILL HELP YOU CRY. Some people have their go-to weepy song list or movie, or a sentimental book that induces tears. If you feel ready and safe to do so, schedule a block of time for you to watch, read, or listen—then reflect. You can invite a special person to experience any of these with you, or you can engage in a solo, cathartic session.

With these tears, I make space for healing.

DECEMBER 13

"The desire of the moth for the star, Of the night for the morrow, The devotion to something afar, From the sphere of our sorrow." —PERCY BYSSHE SHELLEY

Grief often brings with it a sense of longing for something just out of reach. After the loss of a beloved pet, we may find ourselves drawn to memories, places, or dreams that feel both distant and suspended in a world where they still exist beside us.

Shelley's words capture that kind of beautiful ache of losing our beloved pet, the way we reach, like a moth toward a star, for a presence we can no longer hold. This longing doesn't mean we're stuck. It means we're still connected. Our love stretches beyond what's visible, beyond our sorrow, into something sacred and enduring. Grief pulls us inward, but love keeps looking up—toward the light, toward memory, toward meaning.

Though you are beyond my reach, you are never beyond my love.

DECEMBER 14

CREATE A LIGHT-BASED RITUAL. Choose a starlike light to represent your pet's enduring presence. This could be a small LED tealight, a candle, a string of fairy lights, or even a star sticker placed in a meaningful spot. At night, take a moment to turn on, light, or focus on this symbol. As you do, speak or write a message to your pet. It could be as simple as, "I miss you." Let this act be your moth-to-star moment, a way to reach toward the love that still shines. You can do this once or make it part of a weekly ritual. The light becomes a visual reminder that your bond continues to glow beyond grief.

Our bond remains bright, steadfast, and eternal.

DECEMBER 15

"Life is like the moon; now dark, now full." —POLISH PROVERB

The moon itself doesn't change, but as it reflects the sun it appears to wax and wane. We have calendars that chart the phases of the moon so we can know when to catch it in its fullness, or when it's new. The phases of the moon then affect the movement of the tides. Everything on this earth has its rhythm. Although we can't predict how we'll feel from day to day, nor how long grief will last, we do know that our emotions will wax and wane. There will be dark days, and bright days that slowly get brighter. Just because you feel defeated in a moment, it doesn't mean you always will. Reminding ourselves of this will help us adapt to the changes that come with grieving.

My grief will wax and wane, like the natural processes of our solar system.

DECEMBER 16

MAKE A CHANGE IN YOUR LIVING SPACE. Sometimes a change in your environment can help you feel refreshed. This week, consider a few small changes you can make to brighten up your home. You don't have to spend a penny—start by simply rearranging the furniture. If you've been meaning to declutter, sort through some of your belongings and set aside what you can donate. Switch up the books on your coffee table; place a bowl of fresh fruit or flowers on your kitchen table. Not only will you add peace to your home, but you will also have a feeling of accomplishment. Both may boost your mood.

In change, there are inherent elements of cleansing and catharsis, even if we wish they weren't there.

DECEMBER 17

"There isn't much of a rule book on how to grieve for a dog, but I've said a prayer, lit a candle and taken Ella (Mum) for a long walk to spend time remembering Lupo."

—JAMES MIDDLETON, ABOUT ROYAL DOG, LUPO

I once had a client who mentioned he had bought a stuffed animal that resembled the beloved dog he was grieving. When he missed his dog, he'd cuddle the stuffed animal, which made him feel better. He asked, "This is okay, right?" I told him, "It's better than okay; it helps comfort you and that's great. Cuddle away!" There are many similar mourning behaviors that we may feel ashamed of. It's okay to talk to your pet, dream about your pet, or feel their presence. It's okay to want to hug them. This is all part of processing their loss.

I am allowed to seek comfort that feels right to me.

DECEMBER 18

FIND COMFORT HUGGING A STUFFED ANIMAL. According to a 2024 survey of 2,000 adults conducted by Atomik research and commissioned by Build-a-Bear, 40 percent of respondents shared that they sleep with a stuffed animal by their side. This week, consider getting a stuffed animal to hold when you are feeling sad or yearning for your pet. It doesn't have to resemble the same breed or even species as your pet. Just hugging on it can make you feel safe.

I am grateful for how I find ways to feel safe.

DECEMBER 19

"Memory . . . is the diary that we all carry about with us."

—OSCAR WILDE

When we love deeply, we remember through our senses. You might recall your pet's scent; maybe it's still present on a favorite blanket or toy. You may hear their unique sounds in your mind: the trill of a bird, the rhythm of a purr, the padding of paws. You might remember the texture of their fur or scales, the coolness of their nose, or the warmth of their breath. These sensory impressions are the ways our minds and bodies store love.

Research suggests that smell, touch, and taste are harder for most people to recall, especially as time passes, but encountering those sensations again can trigger memories. Many of my clients like to keep items such as pet bedding or clothing that still carry the scent of their pet. Some people also save fur, feathers, or scales they can touch to remember. By consciously holding on to these details, we can revisit them when we need comfort. Like rereading a favorite page in a book, these memories let us feel close to our pets, even after they're gone.

My pet's memory lives in every familiar sense and sensation. I welcome it when I need to.

DECEMBER 20

WHAT ARE YOUR SPECIAL SENSORY MEMORIES? When you feel ready, write about what you remember of your pet with your senses. Think about how they felt, their scent, sounds they made, and their appearance. Spend some time connecting to them: listening to any audio of their sounds, watching a video of them, touching fur that you may have saved, or holding any item that retains their scent.

You are still present in the quiet details of my world.

DECEMBER 21

"All things are literally better, lovelier, and more beloved for the imperfections which have been divinely appointed."

—JOHN RUSKIN

Kintsugi is the Japanese art of repairing broken pottery. Artists use colored lacquer, such as gold, to put the broken pieces back together. Because of the new pattern and streaks of gold, the pottery in its imperfection is very often even more beautiful than the original. In many ways, grieving follows a path like kintsugi. You start out with your heart broken in several pieces, but over time you learn to put the pieces back together, joining them with the golden memories of your beloved pet. In this way, your heart is stronger, though different, and your beloved pet is part of you forever.

I allow myself to change form as I put the fragmented pieces together.

DECEMBER 22

CREATE SOMETHING NEW FROM THAT WHICH WAS BROKEN. This mindful activity of mending pottery can soothe you as you mend your broken heart. Consider exploring the many videos and articles about the process and philosophy of *kintsugi*. If you are interested, look for a local class or investigate available classes online. Alternatively, look around your house and see if there's something you've been meaning to mend or repair. Fixing something and working with your hands can give you a feeling of accomplishment and boost your mood.

DECEMBER 23

"When stars are in the quiet skies,
Then most I pine for thee;
Bend on me then thy tender eyes,
As stars look on the sea!" —EDWARD BULWER-LYTTON

I once knew a family whose four-year-old girl was quite upset at the prospect of losing her dog. The parents told her that if she wanted to talk to her dog after he passed, she could—anytime she liked. He would be in the stars soon, so maybe she could look for signs of him up there. "Will he be with his friends?" the little girl asked. "I imagine they will be there," the parents replied. In the weeks following the pet's passing, the little girl went outside every night to call to her dog. "Hendrix . . . Hendrix . . . Hendrix!" When the first star appeared, she smiled, sure that was him.

In the night, when we are missing our beloved pets, it's possible to take comfort in imagining that they are gazing down upon us like stars over the sea, knowing that a part of them is still shimmering somewhere in the universe.

I am connected to you across time and space.

DECEMBER 24

HONOR YOUR PET'S LEGACY BY PLANTING A TREE OR GROWING A PLANT. If you enjoy gardening, consider growing a plant or young tree in your yard, or getting a new plant for inside your home. Consider naming it after your pet. As your plant grows, consider making cuttings for new plants that you can give as gifts to family or friends in honor of your pet. If you don't enjoy gardening, consider donating a tree in your pet's honor. There are a number of organizations that are planting trees in areas affected by recent wildfires.

I honor your memory through the natural world that will always connect us.

DECEMBER 25

"A gift, though small, is welcome." —HOMER

One of the things you may miss about your relationship with your pet is bringing gifts to them. Providing something extra special for them was another way for you to show your love. If you marked holidays or special occasions with presents, reminding yourself of the joy your presents gave them may help you get through those days more easily. They taught you one of life's most valuable lessons: that there is just as much fulfillment to be found in giving love, as there is in receiving it.

Caring for you was a gift.

DECEMBER 26

REMEMBER THE JOY OF GIVING. What special treats or gifts did your pet enjoy most? Think back to the toys, snacks, or surprises you gave—both on special occasions and just because you loved seeing them happy. If you feel ready, take some time to look at photos or videos of your pet enjoying a gift you gave them. These moments can help reconnect you to the joy and love you shared. On your next holiday or meaningful date, consider honoring that memory by donating a similar gift to a local shelter or offering it to a friend's pet.

Turning your grief into a gesture of kindness is a healing way to carry my love forward.

DECEMBER 27

"Oh, I am very weary, Though tears no longer flow; My eyes are tired of weeping, My heart is sick of woe." —ANNE BRONTË

Grief can be both emotionally and physically exhausting. There may come a point when you feel completely cried out; maybe even your tears are tired. Yet, despite this weariness, sleep may still feel elusive. Many people who are grieving experience disrupted sleep: difficulty falling or staying asleep, restless nights, or drifting off at odd hours during the day.

This disruption can add to the weight of grief, making everything feel harder. Gently guiding yourself back to a nourishing routine by getting consistent rest, staying hydrated, and eating well can help support your body and mind as you heal.

Grieving is hard work. I give myself permission to slow down and restore.

DECEMBER 28

RESET YOUR INNER CLOCK WITH MORNING SUNLIGHT. Absorbing ambient sunlight through our eyes first thing in the morning helps reset our internal clock so we start waking up earlier in the day. As an extra bonus, getting sunlight throughout the day can help you sleep more soundly. Try to get around 30 minutes of sun each day. Don't look directly at the sun; you are just trying to get your eyes exposed to the ambient light. It's okay if it's cloudy. If it's too cold to go outside, you can sit by a window with good sun exposure.

The warmth of the sun reminds me that each day is a chance to reset, to renew, and to care for myself with patience and hope.

DECEMBER 29

"Self-care is one of the active ways that I love myself. When you can and as you can, in ways that feel loving, make time and space for yourself." —TRACEE ELLIS ROSS

The start of a new year has great significance for many people. Many cultures have specific religious customs and traditions to celebrate the new year according to their calendar. The start of a new year is joyful, and a time to prepare for new beginnings. For those of us who are grieving pets, it can be a melancholy time. You are starting a new year without your pet by your side.

While other people around you are making their resolutions and setting goals, all you want is for things to go back to the way they were. One thing that can be helpful is to skip the celebrating and pick a day later in the year as your designated "new beginning." For now, just focus on yourself and your well-being.

I have the power to determine the timing of my own new beginning.

DECEMBER 30

CREATE A "COPING WITH GRIEF" CHEAT SHEET. Sometimes when you are feeling overwhelmed with grief, it's helpful to have a few "go-to" activities at hand that have helped you in the past. Think back through the activities you've tried so far from this book. On an index card or a notes app on your phone, write down the activity and the page it's on. Make sure to keep your cheat sheet handy. Next time you need help coping, take a look at your list and pick an activity. If you have just started this book, you can add new activities as you try things out.

I am always learning new ways to help myself cope.

DECEMBER 31

"For present grief there is always a remedy. However much thou sufferest, hope. The greatest happiness . . . is hope."

—LEOPOLD SCHEFER

I, like many, am no stranger to grief. My first loss was my paternal grandmother, who died when I was four years old. Shortly before her death, she gave me a little cat figurine from her china closet. Whenever I missed my grandmother, I would comfort myself by visiting the china cat, which my mother kept safely on her dresser. Now, more than 60 years later, the little china cat sits on my bookshelf next to a memorial collage of my cat, Joni. I like to think they are watching me as I write this, providing encouragement.

As you experience grief, it's okay to try different "remedies" and skip the ones that don't interest you. Although this is the last entry in the book, it isn't the end. It will be here for you whenever you need to reach for it, to provide healing and hope.

Hope is always within reach.

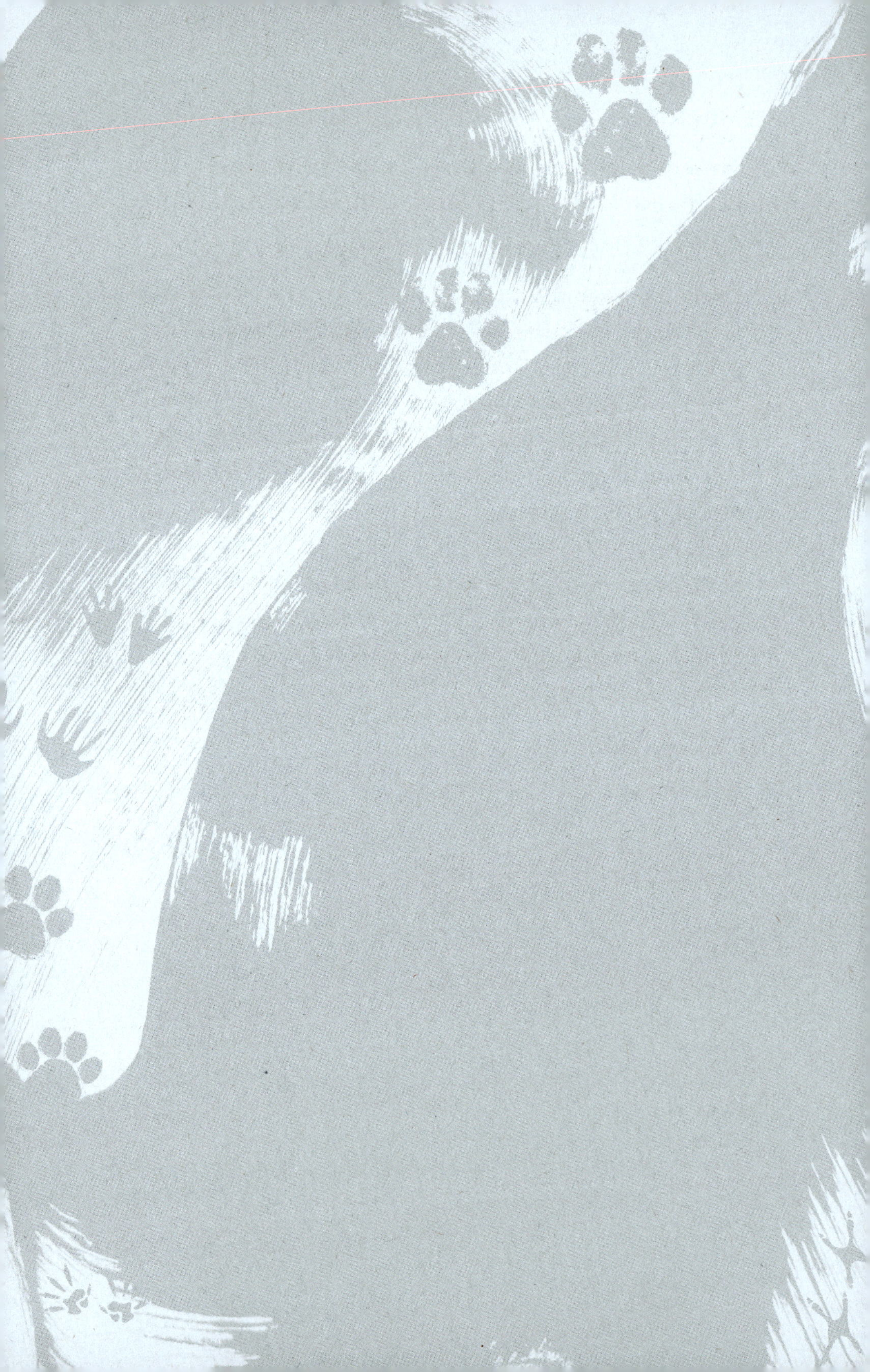

RESOURCES

Websites

WHATSYOURGRIEF.COM – This website's mission is to "promote grief education, exploration, and expression in both practical and creative ways." You will find a ton of resources, articles, online courses, training for grief counselors, a podcast, and a supportive community. They also have a book, listed in the Resources section.

APLB.ORG – The Association for Pet Loss and Bereavement (APBL) was founded in 1997 by Dr. Wallace Sife, author of the pioneering book on pet bereavement, *The Loss of a Pet* (1993). The website offers free online discussion boards for caregivers, online education, a training program for pet counselors, online pet memorials, and a directory of services including counselors and support groups.

PET-LOSS.NET – The Pet Loss Support Page was founded by Moira Anderson Allen, MEd, author of *Coping with Sorrow on the Loss of Your Pet* (2015). The website lists support groups, pet cemeteries, counselors, and other resources. It also has several free printable handouts on a variety of related topics.

PETLOSSHELP.NET – Founded by Susan Stone, LCSW, author of *Mourning Companion Animals: Guiding Clients from Loss to Legacy,* this website offers a memorial hall of fame, individual counseling, counseling training for veterinary practitioners and mental health clinicians, along with other resources.

PETLOSS.COM – Created by Ed Williams in 1995, this website holds an online nondenominational candle ceremony every week, a grief support message board, grief support chat room, helpful articles, and additional links.

RAINBOWSBRIDGE.COM – This website features a pet-loss forum and chat room, educational material, virtual memorials, weekly candle service, and a directory of resources.

MARKSPSYCHIATRY.COM – Dr. Tracey Marks is a psychiatrist with 20+ years' experience on mental health, resilience, and the mind-brain connection. She shares tips on building resilience in the *Resilience Reset Podcast: Science-Based Strategies for Mental Strength.*

THENSF.ORG – Poor sleep is common in people who are grieving. The National Sleep Foundation's website offers education on how you can improve your sleep health and overall well-being. Content on this website breaks down the foundation's research results into knowledge and advice you can apply to your daily sleep routine.

Books

For Adults

Coping with the Loss of a Pet by Christina M. Lemieux, PhD

Coping with Sorrow on the Loss of Your Pet by Moira Anderson Allen MEd.

Children and Pet Loss: A Guide for Helping by Marty Tousley, RN

Going Home: Finding Peace When Pets Die by Jon Katz

The Grief Recovery Handbook for Pet Loss by Russell Friedman, Cole James and John W. James

A 30-Day Guide to Healing from the Loss of Your Pet by Gael J. Ross, LCSW

Bill at Rainbow Bridge by Dan Carrison

Cold Noses at the Pearly Gates by Gary Kurz

The Pet Loss Companion: Healing Advice from Family Therapists Who Lead Pet Loss Groups by Ken Dolan-Del Vecchio and Nancy Saxton-Lopez

When Your Pet Dies: A Guide to Mourning, Remembering, and Healing by Alan D. Wolfelt, PhD

My Pet Remembrance Journal by Enid Traisman

And I Love You Still . . . A Thoughtful Guide and Remembrance Journal for Healing the Loss of a Pet by Julianne Corbin, PhD

General Grief

What's Your Grief?: Lists to Help You Through Any Loss by Eleanor Haley and Litsa Williams

The Grieving Brain by Mary-Frances O'Connor

Notes on Grief by Chimamanda Ngozi Adichie

Mindfulness

The Mindful Self-Compassion Workbook: A Proven Way to Accept Yourself, Build Inner Strength, and Thrive by Kristin Neff, PhD, and Christopher Germer, PhD

Wherever You Go, There You Are by Jon Kabat-Zinn

Self-Help

Get Out of Your Mind and Into Your Life: The New Acceptance and Commitment Therapy by Steven C. Hayes, PhD, with Spencer Smith

The Anxiety and Worry Workbook by David A. Clark, PhD, and Aaron T. Beck , MD

The Worry Cure: Seven Steps to Stop Worry from Stopping You by Robert L. Leahy, PhD

For Children

When a Pet Dies by Fred Rogers

Dog Heaven by Cynthia Rylant

Cat Heaven by Cynthia Rylant

The Tenth Good Thing About Barney by Judith Viorst

Healing Your Grieving Heart for Kids by Alan D. Wolfelt , PhD

Because of Flowers and Dancers by Sandra Brackenridge, LCSW

The Dead Bird by Margaret Wise Brown

The Goodbye Book by Todd Parr

The Invisible Leash by Patrice Karst

Goodbye, Friend: A Journey Through Pet Loss and Grieving: Emotional Healing and Comfort for Parents and Children Experiencing Grief from the Death of a Pet by Owen Whitmore

When Pets Say Goodbye: A Parent's Guidebook for Supporting Children Through Pet Loss by Hayley Jennings

For Professionals

Mourning Companion Animals: Guiding Clients from Loss to Legacy by Susan Dowd Stone, LCSW

Continuing Bonds in Bereavement, edited by Dennis Klass and Edith Maria Steffen

New Techniques of Grief Therapy: Bereavement and Beyond, edited by Robert A. Neimeyer

Grief Counseling and Grief Therapy by J. William Worden

Helplines

CORNELL UNIVERSITY PET LOSS SUPPORT HOTLINE – (607) 218-7457

TUFTS UNIVERSITY PET LOSS SUPPORT HOTLINE – (508) 839-7966

LAP OF LOVE PET LOSS & BEREAVEMENT SUPPORT – (855) 352-5683

CHICAGO VETERINARY MEDICAL ASSOCIATION PET LOSS SUPPORT HOTLINE – (603) 325-1600

UTAH STATE UNIVERSITY PET LOSS SUPPORT HOTLINE – (435) 757-4540

PETFRIENDS – (800) 404-PETS (7387)

988 SUICIDE AND CRISIS LIFELINE: FREE AND AVAILABLE 24/7 – Call or text 988 or visit 988lifeline.org

Support Groups and Counseling

THE INTERNATIONAL ASSOCIATION OF ASSISTANCE DOG PARTNERS – (IAADP.org) offers support for loss of a service dog. Call (816) 237-5541 or email ADLC@iaadp.org with the type of loss you are experiencing, your phone number, and the best time to reach you. A facilitator will call to discuss your needs and if a support group is right for you.

PSYCHOLOGY TODAY – (PsychologyToday.com) provides a "Find a Therapist" feature on their website to search for support groups. Use "pet bereavement" or "pet loss" as keywords. You can also search for individual therapists by location, specialty, and insurance.

LAP OF LOVE – (LapOfLove.com) offers free online pet-loss support groups, pet-loss courses, and individual counseling.

THE GRIEF RECOVERY METHOD – (GriefRecoveryMethod.com) is a six-week online group that uses the material from *The Grief Recovery Handbook for Pet Loss*. They also offer one-on-one grief support.

THE ASSOCIATION FOR PET LOSS AND BEREAVEMENT – (APLB.org) offers free online chat rooms for caregivers and a directory of services including counselors and support groups.

PETCLOUD – (PetCloud.com) offers free online support groups as well as daily support groups with paid membership.

PET LOSS PARTNERS – (PetLossPartners.org) provides virtual pet-loss support groups, chat rooms, and pet bereavement counselor training.

REFERENCES

Brown, Anna. 2023. "About Half of U.S. Pet Owners Say Their Pets Are as Much a Part of Their Family as a Human Member." Pew Research Center, July 7. https://www.pewresearch.org/short-reads/2023/07/07/about-half-us-of-pet-owners-say-their-pets-are-as-much-a-part-of-their-family-as-a-human-member.

Cartwright, Benjamin D. S., Mathew P. White, and Thomas Clitherow. 2018. "Nearby Nature 'Buffers' the Effect of Low Social Connectedness on Adult Subjective Wellbeing over the Last 7 Days." *International Journal of Environmental Research and Public Health* 15 (6): 1238. https://doi.org/10.3390/ijerph15061238.

Descourouez, Mary Grace. 2024. "What Excessive Screen Time Does to the Adult Brain." Stanford Center on Longevity, May 30. https://longevity.stanford.edu/lifestyle/2024/05/30/what-excessive-screen-time-does-to-the-adult-brain.

Hawkins, R. D., and J. M. Williams. 2017. "Childhood Attachment to Pets: Associations Between Pet Attachment, Attitudes to Animals, Compassion, and Humane Behaviour." *International Journal of Environmental Research and Public Health* 14 (5): 490. https://doi.org/10.3390/ijerph14050490.

Herz, Rachel S. 2016. "The Role of Odor-Evoked Memory in Psychological and Physiological Health." *Brain Science* 6 (3): 22. https://doi.org/10.3390/brainsci6030022.

O'Connor, Mary-Frances, and Saren H. Seeley. 2022. "Grieving as a Form of Learning: Insights from Neuroscience Applied to Grief and Loss." *Current Opinion in Psychology* 43: 317–22. https://doi.org/10.1016/j.copsyc.2021.08.019.

Porras-Jiménez, Y. M., P. L. Pancorbo-Hidalgo, I. M. López-Medina, and C. Álvarez-Nieto. "The Role of Laughter Therapy in Adults: Life Satisfaction and Anxiety Control. A Systematic Review with Meta-Analysis." *Journal of Happiness Studies* 26 (99). https://doi.org/10.1007/s10902-025-00934-z.

Shear, M. Katherine. 2010. "Exploring the Role of Experiential Avoidance from the Perspective of Attachment Theory and the Dual Process Model." *Omega*. 61 (4): 357–69. https://doi.org/10.2190/OM.61.4.f.

Tonkin, Lois. 1996. "Growing Around Grief—Another Way of Looking at Grief and Recovery." *Bereavement Care*, 15 (1): 10. https://doi.org/10.1080/02682629608657376.

ACKNOWLEDGMENTS

To my editors at Zeitgeist: Tahra Seplowin for your encouragement and Erin Nelson for your vision and expert edits.

To my sister, Ruth Greenwood, and my brother-in-law, Todd Greenwood, who read the first words of this book and gave me the confidence to write the rest of it. To my nephews, Sebastian and Gabriel, for your love and encouragement.

To my friends who put up with me being too busy to hang out. Your patience and encouraging texts sustained me.

To Neroliza, Luna, and Loren: Abuela Judy can't wait to see you!

To my clients: You taught me so much about bravely managing grief after the loss of a beloved pet, and allowed me to accompany you on that journey,

Thanks to Judith Harbour, Courtney Rabb, and Jamie Cohen at the Schwarzman Animal Medical Center for the opportunity to help your clients and facilitate support groups there.

To El Casinder and Katherine Turman for sharing their love of snakes and horses, respectively.

To Alexio Gessa, for keeping me strong, and Mr. Pauer, for the best music to write to.

And to my sassy cat, ReRe, who curled up next to me as I wrote this book.

ABOUT THE AUTHOR

Judith Eve Rosen, LCSW, is a Beck Institute CBT Certified Clinician based in New York City. She has a virtual private therapy practice and has facilitated pet-loss support groups at the Schwarzman Animal Medical Center of New York. She received her masters in social work from New York University and veterinary social work certification from the University of Tennessee at Knoxville. Prior to her career in social work, Judith was an entertainment journalist and the creator of LaMusica.com, a pioneering website about Latin music. In her spare time, she enjoys theater, good food, and needlework. Judith was born in Detroit and loves cats, which explains why she named her divalicious tortie cat Aretha (ReRe for short) and is a lifelong fan of the Detroit Lions. You can find her on her website, juditheverosen.com, or on Instagram @mypetlosstherapist.

Hi there,

We hope you found *Life After Pet Loss* helpful. If you have any questions or concerns about your book, or have received a damaged copy, please contact customerservice@penguinrandomhouse.com. We're here and happy to help.

Also, please consider writing a review on your favorite retailer's website to let others know what you thought of the book.

Sincerely,

The Zeitgeist Team